"GET YOUR TITS OUT FOR THE LADS"

TRUE STORIES FROM A WOMAN IN FOOTBALL

19/10/2023

"Get Your Tits Out for the Lads"

TRUE STORIES FROM A WOMAN IN FOOTBALL

First published in 2023 by Fair Play Publishing
PO Box 4101, Balgowlah Heights, NSW 2093, Australia
www.fairplaypublishing.com.au

ISBN: 978-1-925914-66-5
ISBN: 978-1-925914-69-6 (ePub)

Cover design and typsetting by Ana Secivanovic
Front cover photograph of Sally Freedman by Sébastien Moret

All inquiries should be made to the Publisher via hello@fairplaypublishing.com.au

CONTENTS

Introduction ... 1

UEFA Euro 2004, Portugal ... 4

It's a Man's World ... 11

The Only Way Is Up … Surely? ... 32

Dreams Do Come True ... 59

Newsfeeds and Sexism ... 67

2022 UEFA Champions League Final, Paris ... 93

(F)unemployment ... 99

A Bittersweet Symphony: 2021 UEFA Women's Euro, England ... 119

The People's Game ... 122

2022 FIFA World Cup, Qatar ... 131

Injury Time Mantra ... 141

Acknowledgements ... 154

Endnotes ... 156

About the Author ... 164

Introduction

When I started working in the wonderful world of football, close friends and family warned me to be really careful. These are some of the comments I heard:

- 'You're going to struggle in a man's world.'
- 'Sally, you're going to need to be very tough.'
- 'Sally, are you sure you can cope?'
- 'Be careful, Sally, there are lots of male, pale dinosaurs running football across the world—you might lose your love for the game.'
- 'You'll need to be very resilient and really strong. You might struggle to get your voice heard.'

Looking back, I was naive, and I immediately dismissed all their concerns:

I will be fine; I love football, I know lots about football. I've grown up with it—playing, watching and coaching. I've got perspectives as a fan, player, coach, writer and from academia. I'll be more than okay. I've got this. Let me live my dream.

I didn't want to believe them. I wanted to make my dream a reality and I wanted it to be a happy one. I didn't want my dream to be tainted in any way—and I certainly didn't believe it would be filled with daily struggles in relation to my gender.

But looking back ... they were right, and I was wrong. Very wrong.

Fast forward to the present—I've been working in sport now for more than 13 years, and in professional football for about eight years—from the 2015 Asian Football Confederation (AFC) Asian Cup to Melbourne City Football Club (FC), to Football Federation Australia (now Football Australia) to Wellington Phoenix FC and the Union of European Football Associations (UEFA).

I have seen little to no improvement in gender equality in this time, and conversely, I have grown more frustrated by the lack of equality and the everyday challenges of being a female in a male-dominated world.

Recently, I began looking back on the many examples of inequality I have experienced. As I reflect, I now understand why my frustration is near breaking point; I have come to the stark realisation that gender discrimination has been taking place throughout my entire career.

After attending the UEFA Euro final in July 2021 between England and Italy at Wembley, I was invited to talk on a Women in Football Australia podcast about my experience as a fan attending the match. Unsurprisingly, we talked a lot about sexism. I spoke passionately about the subject and said, 'Sadly the sexism stories we are hearing and reading about are not isolated events; they happen day in, day out,' and I jokingly claimed, 'I probably have enough stories to write a book!' And at this point I thought to myself that maybe it was time to make writing a book a reality.

I have kept a diary of some of the stories that happened over recent years. Why? Because writing helped me express my thoughts and was a form of escapism—a much-needed release of emotions. Putting pen to paper, or more often than not, hammering my fingers on a keyboard, brought a huge sense of respite and relief. Sexism is not an easy or natural topic to discuss with family, friends or colleagues. In fact, whenever I tried, I found it difficult to be completely honest. I was scared of the backlash—frightened to express my opinion. I constantly thought it would be easier if I stayed quiet, with stiff-upper-lip mode on. The 'I'm fine, I promise' mode. I brushed it under the carpet—all in a frantic effort to 'keep calm and carry on'.

But here I am, revealing all. I am being bold and courageous. I am calling it out. Call it what you want! Yes. It's controversial. But it's also brave. I firmly believe we need to stand up for what we believe in and when respect is no longer being served, we should walk away.

If this book helps one person to gain a better understanding of what it's like to be a woman working in a male-dominated world, I will be happy. And I will be even happier if some readers stop and think about sexism and start to call out sexist behaviour. And if *one person* changes their behaviour as a result of reading this book—then, voilà, I've hit the jackpot!

Lastly, I want to make it clear that this book is not an attack on men. I believe a lot of what has happened to me is not the fault of men, but rather a result of the culture and environment in which we all live, which is (sadly) full of gendered stereotypes. Let's not forget—men and women are fundamentally different which makes it hard for women to put themselves in the shoes of men, and similarly, it is extremely difficult for men to put themselves in the shoes of women.

But this doesn't mean we should not speak up and try to effect change. I know if we stay silent, nothing will change. I think we can all do better—together we are stronger.

Chapter 1

UEFA Euro 2004, Portugal

In June 2004, I went to Portugal with a group of friends to follow England for the first time in a major international tournament. Excited was an understatement! I travelled with five friends: four males and one female, Lisa. On arrival in Lisbon, the carnival atmosphere spread instantly—the sunshine, the noise, the bright colours and the party vibe; people from all over the world, young and old, were jumping for joy, dancing with delight and smiling like they didn't have a care in the world.

Not long after arriving at the bustling main square in Lisbon, I took a step back and watched on in awe. I remember thinking to myself, *wow, the power of football is quite remarkable, look at all these people—here for one common reason and despite being strangers, they are celebrating together like friends.* Football really is one of the few common languages in the world.

The sun shone brightly, and blue skies set the scene for an unforgettable two weeks. Within only a few days, I was convinced I wanted more. I was hooked. Without hesitation, I remember telling my friends, 'I want more; let's all go to Germany for the World Cup in 2006, with tickets or without!'

June 13, 2004, England v France, Estádio da Luz, Lisbon

One sunny, hot afternoon, the guys in the group went ahead of Lisa and I to a bar before the big match between England and France in

Lisbon. Lisa and I arranged to meet our friends at the bar a bit later on in the day. A couple of hours passed, and we set off to start our first adventure ... no need for Google Maps—we simply followed the raucous noise coming from the fans!

As kick-off approached, the excitement built. England fans were in full voice with beers aplenty as they basked in the scorching sunshine in anticipation of the big match ahead. As we approached the bar, we needed to somehow navigate our way across a crazy, chaotic, traffic-filled, busy main road. We were waiting cautiously to cross, looking left, looking right, when one or two guys in the crowded bar noticed us from afar. And almost immediately, without any hesitation, they pointed in our direction and started the chant, 'Get your tits out for the lads!'

Within a few seconds, it had gone from one or two guys to hundreds of men, singing deafeningly whilst simultaneously pointing and staring right at us. We looked at each other sheepishly; we were so embarrassed! 'Now what do we do?' Lisa asked.

'Well, we need to get to the bar, so I guess, we go forth and conquer—and cross the road!' I said.

And with that, once it was safe, we skipped across the road. Time stood still. All eyes were now firmly on us. As we approached, the noise became thunderous, the cheers and jeers got louder and louder. I covered my ears to try and soften the sound—it was ear-piercing! As we finally entered the bar, we were greeted by every man and his dog—all of them singing in unison without a care in the world—as they performed a final, roaring-crescendo rendition of the notorious chant, 'Get your tits out for the lads!'

A bit of harmless fun? Don't get me wrong, at the time, we were smiling ... but let's take stock. Can you imagine if it had been the other way round? Let's imagine hundreds of women in a bar, and two guys approach ... would the ladies start singing, 'Get your cocks out for the girls!'? Of course not. Funny that, isn't it?

But if nothing else, to all the lads in that bar, thank you from the bottom of my heart!

What for?

For my book title!

2007

I moved from England to Australia when I received the only full academic scholarship to study a Master of Business specialising in Sport Management at Griffith University. Within the first few weeks, I joined a five-a-side, social, mixed futsal competition and I was happy to be playing futsal two to three times every week. I loved it. Well, apart from the strange rules: each team had to have a minimum of two girls. OK—that's a good start, but once again, we were the minority. Add to the mix that every goal scored by a girl counted for two and every other goal needed to be scored by a girl; in other words, if a male scored, the next goal needed to be a girl's goal. Are you still with me? It took me a while to understand too! I remember being a little bit puzzled and asking the referee, 'Why are there these strange rules, it's a bit like a handicap for girls?'

'It's simple, Sally—without these rules, the girls would never get the ball—the boys won't pass to the girls, so we made girls' goals count for two—to encourage the boys to pass!'

I hated the rules. Why? Because it was reinforcing the perception that girls can't play football as well as boys. I suggested that perhaps it would be better if we were treated equally. After all, a goal is a goal and maybe we could remind the males that football is a team sport—any team using only three male players probably wasn't going to win much anyway. But my comments went unheard, and the rules continued year after year.

You know what happened? Boys did start to realise how important girls were to their teams; instead of playing in one team, I was often asked to fill in and compete in many other teams because several teams couldn't find enough girls to play. Why? I'm not sure, but here are my best guesses:

- Maybe some girls didn't want to play with boys?
- Maybe some girls felt intimidated by the physicality of the boys?
- And maybe the girls didn't have the opportunity to play as younger girls, so they were not confident about their level of ability.

When I suggested that perhaps there should be some consideration of starting an all-female competition, the response was, 'Oh, but Sally, there aren't even enough girls interested to have two in a team. We would never be able to find enough girls for an all-female competition.'

I also played 11-a-side football in Australia for a few different clubs and there were challenges there too. Most commonly, the frequent lack of changing facilities available for girls. On arrival at the fields:

'Oh, we are so sorry, the boys have the change rooms, you'll need to change in the toilet or in your car.'

Or ...

'Oh, sorry, the boys will be out in 10 minutes, so once they're finished, you can enter.' In other words, in the meantime, just wait outside in the sweltering sun and then you can enter a nice dirty, sweaty, muddy change room. How lovely.

And once you're inside, here's your kit—a lovely, second-hand, ancient, oversized men's kit. And where would we play? On the far field, far away—you know, the one with divots and holes, the one on a slope, the field with no draining, no markings, the one with the rusty 'hand-me-down' broken goals with holes in their nets, the pitch that clearly was set aside for the 'little side events', otherwise known as women's football. And this was in 2007.

Rewind to 2003

I first started playing football in Norwich in England in 2003. And you know what, it was the same there too. Oversized hand-me-down men's kits and the pitches we played on were better known as mud swamps. And I was 23.

I was twenty-three years old, and it was the first time playing 11-a-side football had been presented to me as an option. And the opportunity came about by chance. I was watching England play football in the pub. I was occasionally shouting at the television, sometimes telling the players what they should and shouldn't be doing! A girl approached me who I didn't know and said something along the lines of, 'You seem to know a lot about football, would you like to play in our team? We need new players.'

My reply was, 'Oh, I love watching football, but I've never really played other than in the garden with my brothers and at the park.'

'Don't worry, you'll be fine. All abilities welcome. We are a new team and lots of the other girls have never played before either.'

And with that, I said, 'OK, why not!'

Me. 2003. Modelling a lovely Hainford ladies FC hand me down oversized men's kit.

That's me in 2003. I'm sporting one of those much-talked-about, lovely, hand-me-down men's kits. From memory, I rolled the waistband on the shorts (which were the smallest ones) at least three times in order for them to semi-resemble shorts rather than three-quarter-length somethings, the smallest-sized socks constantly fell down, as (guess what) my calves are not as big as men's, and the sleeves were long enough to keep my freezing hands slightly warm (one bonus)!

After only a couple of training sessions, I heard some dreaded words from the coach: 'If only you had started playing when you were younger, Sally, you could have been exceptional.' OK, maybe 'dreaded' is harsh. The words were lovely, and the intention was good. But it made me angry. Why? Because I never had the opportunity to try. Most likely, I would not have been exceptional, but I will never know and nor will thousands of other girls my age.

So now it's time to say a big thank you to Lucy. Without meeting Lucy in the pub one night in Norwich I would have never started playing 11-a-side football.

My Instagram post from September 2019 says all you need to know.

From left to right: Sally, Emily and Lucy at UEFA Headquarters, Nyon Switzerland

I met these amazing girls in 2003 in the pub in Norwich watching England... Thanks to these girls, an amazing coach and a great club, I became even more fond of the beautiful game.

Sixteen years later, here we are reunited in Nyon, standing on the roof of @uefa HQ. Thanks for visiting, girls. Very grateful I met you that night and so grateful you gave me little choice in joining Hainford Ladies FC. The most enjoyable, fun football club on the planet! Cheers to football and friends xx

Why is this so important?

Throwback to 1987

I asked to play football at school in 1987, when I was seven years old. And the response? My PE teacher said, 'Football is only for boys, Sally. You can play hockey or netball.'

When I rebelled and went to the boys' side of the playground to play football (yes, we had a girls' side and boys' side of the playground), I was punished and told to stand on the line. Punished for playing football. The boys could play. The girls could not.

Chapter 2

It's a Man's World

In 2007, I completed my application to study a Master of Business (Sport Management) at Griffith University in Brisbane, Australia. When I applied, I was asked to outline what I would like to research and what I would like to change. Within minutes of starting the application form, my words were flowing.

I wanted to research why girls were not provided with the same opportunities as boys when it came to playing football. As a result of my proposed research, I wanted to make some recommendations to bring equality to the sport. I remember discussing my application with a study agency who were helping me collate all the necessary documents. They were honest. 'Sally, normally this one scholarship is awarded to a PhD student who is studying science, maybe researching a cure for a disease, but by all means, you can try and submit your application about girls' football—you never know, but I think your chances are slim!'

Three months after submitting my lengthy application, an email arrived in my inbox: '*Congratulations, you have been awarded a full academic scholarship to study at Griffith University.*' I almost fell off the chair!

In July 2007, I set off on an adventure which was meant to last one year. It lasted eleven-and- a-half years!

After graduating with a high distinction, three awards for academic excellence and a Grade Point Average of 6.7, coupled with three years' professional business management experience in the United Kingdom, I thought I might have a reasonable chance of securing a role in football administration in Australia. I applied for many. I had coffee after coffee with key stakeholders. And each time, I was faced with these old classic chestnuts:

- 'You're too experienced for us.'
- 'We can't afford to pay you what you deserve.'
- 'I don't think a career in football is suitable for you.'
- 'Maybe look at other industries that aren't so male-dominated.'
- 'You're too intelligent to work in football. Your talent will be wasted.'
- 'You'll be surrounded by male, sexist dinosaurs.'

Too experienced? I was 27 years *young*. I had only ever had one professional, full-time job on a graduate leadership scheme for an insurance company, and I had a BSc Honours degree in Psychology and now a Master of Business. And that made me too experienced? Wow.

Despite all my efforts, I was unable to find a role within football or sport, so I started to look elsewhere. Eventually, I was offered a role as business manager for an economic consulting firm. Not quite the football career I dreamed of, but hey, it was a job and it meant I could stay in Australia.

My sport career started in 2010 when I finally got a break in, sadly, not football, but ice skating. Yes, ice rinks do exist in Australia! I was employed as business manager for Ice Skating Queensland. It was far from ideal, but it was at least a role in sport. And I thought it could be a good stepping-stone. I made a leap of faith—crossed my fingers and thought, let's give it a go!

It turned out to be the right move as from there my career in sport took off. A few jobs followed—marketing manager for a large fitness complex; area director for an international gym; business development manager for a top university's sport department and then finally, the football dream became a reality—I was offered a permanent job as protocol manager for the AFC Asian Cup in 2015!

I had applied to be a volunteer at the Asian Cup, and I was invited to attend a volunteer assessment at a centre in Brisbane in 2014. At the time, I was in Brazil for the World Cup. Fortunately, I was due to land in Brisbane about two hours before the start time for the volunteer session. After an exhausting 40 hours of travel, I rushed home, showered, jumped in my car, and I arrived just on time for the assessment. I was extremely jet-lagged, irritable and tired, but strangely I was also full of energy, and I couldn't shut up about the magical World Cup experience I had just had in Brazil.

The last part of the assessment centre meeting involved a 10-minute, one-on-one chat with someone from the Brisbane venue team. We had to pick a queue and wait our turn. When I got to the front, I was greeted by the venue manager for Brisbane; she asked me a few quick-fire, standard interview questions. I answered all with bounds of enthusiasm and from memory, I threw in a few too many stories about Brazil and also my beloved Brighton and Hove Albion (the team I have followed from childhood).

The next day, I received a phone call: 'Sally, we were so impressed with you, your football knowledge, your experience and your raw passion—would you be interested in applying for the permanent protocol manager role we are currently recruiting for?'

'Sorry, what's a protocol manager?

'It's VIP and VVIP management—you would be responsible for looking after government officials, princes, princesses, the lord mayor, the Prime Minister, the families of the players and so on.'

'Oh, I see. Umm. OK. That sounds interesting. Sure. Hang on, did you say there are VIPs and VVIPs? What's the difference?'

'Don't worry about that now—but yes, there are very important people and then there are the very, very important people.'

And with that, I did a bit more research and then submitted my application. And a couple of interviews later, the job offer arrived in my inbox. But Houston ... we had a problem!

What?

I had just started a role at the University of Queensland as business development manager for their sport department, which I was really enjoying. Yet, at the same time, I had been waiting so long for a football opportunity to arrive—what to do? Where there is a will, there is a way!

I decided I was going to ask my boss (the CEO of University of Queensland Sport) if I could go on sabbatical to complete the Asian Cup role. Before asking the big question, I thought it would be best if I went in prepared with an all-singing, all-dancing presentation to sell the benefits. And with my head now spinning at one hundred miles per hour, sleep was out of the question, so instead, I stayed up most of the night and prepared a presentation outlining the benefits that my proposed sabbatical could potentially bring to the university.

The next morning arrived, and I bounced into the office at the crack of dawn. As soon as the CEO was in the building, I knocked on his office door. He told me he was busy and asked if I could come back at 5 p.m. I went back to my desk ... but I couldn't possibly wait until 5 p.m. to ask this. I knocked again and asked for five minutes and explained it was really important. He welcomed me into his office. Only two minutes or so into my lengthy presentation, my manager told me to 'Stop.' I thought, *uh oh ... what have I done here?* But in fact, he didn't need to hear anymore.

He told me, 'Of course you can go, why would I stop you? And if this helps you secure your dream job at UEFA or FIFA, I am more than happy to help.'

I was so excited and extremely grateful.

And so off I went to work at the AFC Asian Cup in 2015. I had the green light to go forth and conquer. My rollercoaster football ride began!

LinkedIn Post, April 22, 2015

'From the day I went to study a Master's in Business (Sport Management) in Australia in 2007, I only ever had one ultimate goal. I was determined to land a dream job in football. I was a fan, a player and a coach and loved the beautiful round ball game more than most things!

Fast forward to October 2014 and finally, my dream became a reality; after applying to be a volunteer for the AFC Asian Cup Australia 2015, I somehow impressed enough to be offered a football fan's dream: a paid role as protocol manager for Brisbane. Ironically, at the time, I

Asian Cup 2015, Brisbane, Australia

didn't even know what a protocol manager did! I quickly understood that I would be responsible for VIPs and VVIPs (yes, there are Very Important People and then there are the Very, Very Important People) across the hotels, stadium, airport and all events associated with the largest sporting event Australia had hosted since the Olympics in 2000. From princes to princesses, to chairmen, to presidents, to CEOs, the list of VVIPs was undeniably scary, but as the name-dropping continued, it rapidly made me realise that this really was a once-in-a-lifetime opportunity that I categorically had to say yes to.

At the time of the offer, I was employed by the University of Queensland (UQ) Sport as Business Development Manager. UQ quickly recognised that this opportunity was something I had dreamed of, and without any hesitation allowed me to embark on a sabbatical to work for the AFC Asian Cup Australia.

Two months since the conclusion of the cup, I look back with immense pride. The highs were off the scale and I have memories that will certainly stay with me forever. By the same token, the lows were some of the toughest days I have experienced in my career to date. I learnt so much in such a short period of time that despite nearly tearing my hair out on a few occasions, I am now certain that the hard work and ridiculously long hours were worth it.

October 2014 / Goodbye UQ, hello Asian Cup

Witnessing the spectacular ending emphasised this further; seeing Australia lift the winning silverware after a thrilling final against South Korea in front of near on 80,000 fans on home soil was an occasion to savour. At the outset, so many people doubted the event would be a success.

Eddie McGuire (established TV sports presenter and AFL pundit) foolishly described the event as a possible 'lemon'. I'm not sure a 'lemon' is the most appropriate label for an event which saw over 670,000 fans (double the expected crowd) attend 32 matches across Sydney,

Australia vs. South Korea, Asian Cup Final 2015

Canberra, Newcastle, Brisbane and Melbourne (with an average match attendance figure of 21,000). In my opinion, we can forget the lemon and instead crack open the Moet. The AFC Asian Cup Australia is expected to announce figures of surplus in excess of $20 million when the final audit is completed next week, despite fears the event would break even at best. Who looks like a lemon now?!

Incredibly, beyond all expectations, 9 of the 32 matches sold out completely. It came as no surprise then when the AFC President described the AFC Asian Cup Australia 2015 as the 'best Asian Cup ever'. Frank Lowy, FFA Chairman, echoed his sentiment and said, 'I think it's a fantastic boost for us in Australia, in Asia and around the world, everybody will take notice of us.'

Having worked in sport for the last six years, I can say with confidence that this experience is the most rewarding thing I've completed in sport. I love football more than most, and sadly, as most of my friends keep reminding me, I support my local team, Brighton and Hove Albion FC. They only just managed to avoid relegation this season, meaning the 2014/15 season is one I definitely want to forget. Conversely, the memories I gained from working at the AFC Asian Cup Australia in 2014 and 2015 are memories that I will treasure forever.'

What Were the Lows?

There were a couple of occasions where I was unable to do parts of my job as certain VVIP guests refused to be met by a woman due to their religious and/or cultural beliefs. However, as I was the only person granted permission to carry a swipe card to allow VVIP vehicles into the stadium, my job suddenly became tricky when I was abruptly 'not welcome' in the vicinity. We found a workaround, and somehow made it happen. However, I felt incredibly frustrated that I couldn't do certain elements of my job just because I was a woman.

It was the start. I began to feel invisible for the first time.

Unsurprisingly, the VIP and VVIP lounges were dominated by men which made things interesting and memorable; on the first match day, one vivid memory I have is when two senior male staff members had to be physically separated by stadium security staff after an extremely loud, chaotic, visible altercation. I won't go into details of why, what, where or who. But it was an eye-opener and one that meant instead of going home at midnight, I was working at the stadium until around 3 a.m. taking phone calls and writing reports.

You probably won't be surprised to read that when people around me started to describe their version of events, they repeatedly said words along the lines of ... 'Don't worry, Sally, it was just men being men.' 'Men and their egos. Don't worry about it.' Oh, silly me. That makes it OK then. I will write those exact words in my report, and I won't worry anymore. And instead, I'll look forward to more fights. I cannot wait. More of the same tomorrow, please.

Coaching Under-16 Boys—2015

My friends thought I was mad:

- 'You're going to coach under 16 boys' football?'
- 'Are you sure? They will be so mean to you.'
- 'They won't take you seriously.'
- 'Boys at that age are cheeky. They are rude.'
- 'The boys might not respect you simply because you're a woman.'
- 'And you're doing this for free? Why? Don't be so silly. It's so time consuming.'

I ignored all the comments and committed to coaching the University of Queensland under-16 boys' team. I knew there would be challenges. I knew it wouldn't be easy. But a coach is a coach, right? It shouldn't matter if they are female or male. I was more qualified than some; I had an English FA Level 1 coaching qualification, I had played football for eight years, I had watched many matches from grassroots to professional football all around the world, I had coached young girls and boys previously in England and according to my trainers who taught me how to coach, I had 'outstanding communication skills and an exceptional coaching style'.

Thankfully, it wasn't as bad as I feared. But one thing I do remember is how hard I had to work to earn respect. At first, the boys were outwardly unconvinced, doubtful and unsure:

- 'Are you sure about this, Sally?'
- 'Do you really think that?'
- 'How long did you play football for?'
- 'Who do you support?'
- 'Do you even know what "offside" means?'
- 'Can you show us that trick, Sally?'
- 'Can you pass the ball that far, Sally? I bet you can't.'

I was on trial and being tested from the moment I arrived at my first few training sessions to the moment I left them.

But after only a few sessions, the boys quickly began to welcome me with open arms. We were winning more than we were losing, which helped. And eventually, training was far from a chore. It was a pleasure. The team finished second.

So, to all those budding female coaches out there—go for it. Don't be afraid to step into a 'man's world'. Just be prepared to work harder than your male counterparts to 'earn your stripes'.

If we get more females coaching, hopefully we will see articles about top European coaches with women featured. I saw one article in November 2022 from UEFA with the title '*Top UEFA European Club Coaches Attend UEFA Forum*'. The accompanying headline image? Seven white men.[1]

What a truly inspiring image for any up-and-coming female coaches out there.

Don't believe me that it really is a man's world? Keep reading.

Women in the Workforce

A friend living in the Netherlands recently sent me an article with the title:

'Is the Part-Time Working Woman a Spoiled Part-Time Princess or a Cinderella?'

'What? Where? Why?' I asked.

I received this explanation:

'A 'part-time princess' is a saying we use in the Netherlands—it sums up the image of women working a few hours before going out for lunch with friends or pursuing their hobby, and then they start drinking white wine in the mid-afternoon. But if they just put in a few more hours, all the problems would go away.'

'Oh gosh,' I said. 'That sounds horrendous and actually, so many female jobs are often more suited to part-time—like education or care.'

'Yes, that is right and that's why they become overworked and undervalued; as more women enter a certain profession, salary and prestige decrease.'

'Oh gosh,' I said again. 'It's a horrible, vicious cycle. We cannot win.'

My friend went on to tell me that the article mentioned that women were less likely to be given the benefit of the doubt when applying for jobs, they often have to prove themselves for longer to progress and are less likely to climb the career ladder. And if they do make it, they likely have poorer conditions and less money than their male colleagues.

'Sounds extremely familiar,' I said.

The article went on to describe that at the same time, women at work often have the largest share of 'invisible' tasks—those which are often exhausting and emotionally taxing: thankless administrative or practical chores, like assisting colleagues, students or patients with emotional problems or organising social activities.

'Funny you say that,' I said. 'One of my female friends recently told me it took her a whole day to get through school administration paperwork for her two sons. An excursion trip form here, some homework forms there, a health vaccine form, a medical certificate here and so on. It never stops.'

And when you think it can't get much worse, the majority of unpaid informal care comes down to ... you guessed it—women.

'So, basically it sucks to be a woman?' I suggested.

'Yes,' my friend replied. 'We do all the "crap" and yet there is less confidence in our abilities, less appreciation for our contribution and we get paid less!'

'So did the article have any solutions?' I asked.

It did.

'Women will benefit more from structurally equal career opportunities, rewards and bonuses, and higher salaries for "women's professions". In addition, they deserve better working conditions in which "invisible" work is also distributed and rewarded equally.

'Finally, employers should do more to make it easier to combine work and family responsibilities and to facilitate informal care. For example, by having meals delivered at home or offering a free laundry, cleaning or babysitting service.

'Because anyone who expects women to work more hours should start by treating them not as Cinderellas, but as fully fledged employees.'

The article's author was Naomi Ellemers (an organisational and social psychologist and professor at Utrecht University).[2]

And then, just like magic, this popped up on my LinkedIn newsfeed.

'Unlocking the Full Potential of Women in the Economy'

Anne Hathaway is Goodwill Ambassador for UN Women. She gave a speech at the B20/G20 Indonesia Summit in November 2022. Here are some extracts which resonated:

'Women's participation and equal power is fundamental to progress for everyone. I'm sure you are aware of the evidence which shows conclusively that equality between women and men makes us all safer, happier, more prosperous, and more successful. And yet, the reality in which we find ourselves is that at the current rate of progress, it may take another 300 years to achieve gender equality. I hope we all agree that this is three centuries too long.

'Our current position is far from good. Progress for women and girls is in dramatic reverse in many countries. Rights and freedoms that women and girls had experienced as normal—to work, to learn, to make choices about their bodies—have been abruptly taken away.

'Millions of women left the workforce in 2020, they lost their jobs at faster rates than men and have stayed out of the job market longer.

'Ironically, the pandemic also showed us just how much our future progress depends on the skills and leadership of women. Women sustained our healthcare systems and invented lifesaving vaccines. As

leaders of countries, they gave us some of the most effective responses to the pandemic.

'And yet, we show time and time again that we do not equally value women's participation, contribution, and leadership.

'This year, in 169 countries and areas (that's most of the world), women's labour force participation is expected to stay below pre-pandemic levels.

'Why is this?

'During the pandemic, women did an additional 512 billion hours of unpaid care work at home.

'However, we must also recognize the reality that the current way care is provided and valued is unfair and unsustainable. We must address the cultural biases that automatically label care as "women's work".

'Even before the pandemic women spent more than three times as many hours as men on unpaid care and domestic work. It was unfair then, it's worse now. It's time to admit something is very, very off.

'Whether or not we mean to, the fact is, we are taking advantage of women ... We must stop penalising women for caring.

'UN Women has observed that care that's appreciated and properly valued in all its forms is a critical missing link in unlocking the full potential of women in the economy and in society, which is, of course, the same thing as unlocking the full potential of everyone in the economy and society. Governments, businesses, and civil society can all play a role in this.

'UN Women would like to propose these practical and immediate actions:

'Ask governments to support care services. Pay the taxes that fund them.

'Prioritise the creation of family friendly workplaces which include flexible working hours, paid parental leave, and in-house childcare facilities.

'This is a moment when we must urgently act not only to restore what has been lost for women and girls but to end the harmful status quo which keeps inequality thriving.

'The stakes simply couldn't be higher. The world—not just

women—needs innovative solutions more than ever. Optimising inclusivity is our best chance at success.

'I urge you to put women at the heart of economic growth and recovery. Be the architects of a better future by doing what no one has effectively done before:

'Prioritise women for the good of all.'[13]

In November 2022, the European Union posted this on Equal Pay Day:

'Equal work deserves equal pay: this is a founding principle of the European Union.

'However, women in the European Union still continue to earn less than men for equal jobs. They earned on average 13% less than men last year, meaning that for every €1 a man earned, a woman earned €0.87.

'Today, we symbolically mark #EqualPay day to highlight the date when women stop getting paid compared to their male colleagues, on an annual basis. In other words, from today onwards, it is as if women were working for free.

'This has to change. That is why we are doubling down our efforts on gender equality and the root causes of pay inequality, in particular with ambitious legislations on:

- *pay transparency*
- *gender balance on corporate boards*
- *minimum wages for workers*
- *work-life balance*

Because everyone benefits, when all are equal.'[14]

And in December 2022, the European Parliament posted that a deal had been reached on binding pay-transparency measures and that European Union companies will be required to disclose information on salaries to expose gender pay gaps. The provisional agreement stipulates that those workers and workers' representatives will have the right to receive clear and complete information on individual and average pay levels, broken down by gender. Pay secrecy will be banned: there should be no contractual terms that restrict workers from disclosing their pay, or from seeking information about the same or other categories of workers' pay.'[5]

It felt good to see that my thoughts and feelings were backed by research and statistics, albeit some ones which suggest we are going backwards, rather than forwards.

Melbourne City FC

With multiple sport roles and the Asian Cup on my CV, I started to search for a role in Australia within football once again. Quite quickly, I was offered a role as head of fan engagement for Melbourne City FC (part of the City Football Group). Without much hesitation, I accepted. It meant saying cheerio to the warm, sunshine State of Queensland which had been home for seven years and hello to the rainy and cold State of Victoria!

Like most jobs, there were lots of highs and some memorable lows.

The most shocking low still sends chills to my spine. It was said to me during a post-match fan function as I tried to escort a player onto the stage. As I ushered him through the crowds, I joked with some fans, 'He's only small, coming through.' And the player's response? To whisper in my ear, *'My cock is f"*!ing massive and wouldn't you like to see it?'*

What a lovely thing to say to any woman, let alone a work colleague.

What did I say? What did I do? Nothing. I simply carried on with my job.

Did I tell anyone at the club? No. Why? Because I didn't think I would be taken seriously, and I was also quite new to the job and club. I was scared and apprehensive to speak up. I didn't want to create a 'storm'. And I didn't believe anything would change if I did say anything. I thought there would be zero punishment and most likely it would be brushed under the carpet.

Perhaps I was wrong. Looking back, perhaps I should have been braver and raised my voice. After all, if we stay silent, nothing will ever change. But at the time, my instinct took over. I laughed it off, tried to stay calm and attempted to carry on like nothing had happened.

Office Politics

I was asked to attend a one-on-one meeting at short notice. I was told in this meeting that 'all staff were being talked to about what happened last night'. I was a little confused as I hadn't been out the night before, so I didn't really know what was being referred to, but off I went to the meeting that was deemed 'urgent'.

As it turned out, a few staff had been out the night before celebrating with some players and it got a little out of hand. Consequently, all staff were being reminded of their obligations and responsibilities as staff members of City Football Group. I listened and explained I wasn't there, but I understood. I asked if I should pass the same message on to my two team members. I was told there was no need. A couple of weeks later, I asked my team members (one male and one female, neither of whom were involved in the incident) if they had been given the same chat I received. The female team member had. The male team member had nothing said to him.

Eleven Months Later: 'We are terribly sorry, Sally. Your job no longer exists.'

In 2016, the position I was working in (head of fan engagement) was made redundant. It was unexpected, but it's life. Naturally, I was disappointed. I had only recently moved to Melbourne, and I had no inkling it was coming.

Onwards and upwards. I tried to remain optimistic.

On the plus side, I had created some networks within the football family, and I was hopeful that another opportunity would present itself. After working at the AFC Asian Cup in Australia in 2015, I contacted a senior staff member at the AFC to ask if they knew of any suitable roles for the 2019 AFC Asian Cup which was to be hosted in Dubai in the United Arab Emirates.

Suffice to say, my contact told me that there would be little chance of finding a role, as the local organising committee was "dominated by men as a common practice in the Middle East".

2017: From Calm, Considered and Kind, to Anger, Shock and Disbelief

I think those who know me would agree that I am generally a happy, easy-going, calm and considerate person, and to turn these traits on their head would take something big.

When you're female, using a female toilet shouldn't be difficult, right?

I was attending training at a stadium. My role was to take photos, interview and film a couple of players, and promote our upcoming match on social media. I was going to be present at the stadium for around two hours. On arrival, I needed to use the bathroom. I went to the ladies—it was locked. I found the facilities manager of the stadium and asked if he could please open the ladies' bathroom. The response I received: 'No, you can just use the men's.' I couldn't quite believe what I was hearing.

I said, 'Pardon?'

He replied, 'You can just use the men's bathroom, save us cleaning the ladies' one.'

I was in shock. Why? Because he appeared to think it was reasonable for me to use the men's bathroom. And why was this so terrible? Because if I followed his lackadaisical instructions, I would have walked through the male dressing room (where the team were currently getting changed), and then strolled into an open-plan male bathroom with urinals and showers (because that's not awkward at all). If I survived that little adventure, I could maybe find a free private male cubicle and pee! And to exit, I'd need to do the same in reverse.

I took a second to take stock and, admittedly, in a slightly raised voice, I replied, 'No, I cannot—you can *just* open the ladies' bathroom. I am a female, and I am going to be working here for most training sessions, so can you please open the female bathroom and make sure it is open for future sessions too?'

A blank, stunned face looked back at me, but still no words. I went one step further ...

'I will not walk into a male bathroom full of urinals where there are men. But if you really insist, I will go there and put my used sanitary pad down the men's toilet. Last time I checked, male toilets did not have sanitary bins. And I'm pretty sure a blocked toilet is going to cost you more time and money to fix than the time and money it takes you to open the ladies. It's not rocket science; open the female toilet, please.'

And with that, the facilities manager reluctantly tramped off to get the key, and some 10 minutes later, he opened the door.

Fast forward a week and I was at the stadium again ... and guess what? You know what's coming. I knew what was coming. Yes, you guessed it. The female toilets were locked. As I pushed the door handle down and leant against the door to double check, the negative thoughts came flooding right back—*wow, women really don't exist in this world. I cannot even go to the bathroom.*

I fell against the door and sank to the floor. I didn't want to do this job anymore. I sat in a ball, grasping my knees tightly with my head burrowed; I wanted the ground to swallow me. Enough now. I'm done.

It was something seemingly so trivial, but when it happens time and time again, my patience wears thin; the mini battles were starting to rapidly accumulate and becoming exhausting. I felt invisible. Why do I have to fight so hard to exist in this male-dominated football world?

Sadly, I had many similar experiences at other stadiums and events; on many occasions, the only open bathrooms were the male toilets. Apparently, all to save some cleaning money and/or because women don't work in football—or if we do, we are an afterthought, or worse still, we are unseen, and in any case, ladies can apparently 'just' use the men's toilets.

It got me thinking about what matters. *How did we get here?* A few topics came to mind:

- language
- search engines
- stereotypes
- media articles
- masculinity and femininity.

Let's look at each one in turn.

Language Matters

Isn't it strange that in English we have Miss, Mrs and Ms to denote whether a female is married or not, yet for men it's only Mr? Is it just me or is it peculiar that women are asked each and every time they complete a form to declare to the world if they are married or single? Or, if women would like to be mysterious and keep people guessing, they can choose Ms. Yet, for men, there is a one-size-fits-all—Mr.

Maybe it's not a big deal. Perhaps I am overthinking, but I am curious to know why it's like this. Personally, I am often torn between Miss and Ms—I am single, but then on some days I think to myself, why does it matter? On those days, I'll select Ms because, firstly, it's none of your business whether I am single or married, and secondly, this information (unless I am missing something) has absolutely no purpose.

Search Engines Matter

I remember when a colleague working in sport shared a post on LinkedIn that summed up what it's like to be living in a world designed by men, for men. She searched for something related to the UEFA Women's Champions League. And then, Google asked her if what she really meant was the UCL (the men's League)? I mean, why would anyone want to know about the Women's Champions League, Google?

Her post read*:*

'There's a broader point to made about the need for rights holders and technology platforms to prioritise and support women's sport, rather than optimising their activity based on historic behaviour that occurred during a time that massively favoured and benefited men's sport/I could talk about that all day, but for the time being, no, Google, I did not mean Juventus Chelsea UCL Group Stage MD2.'

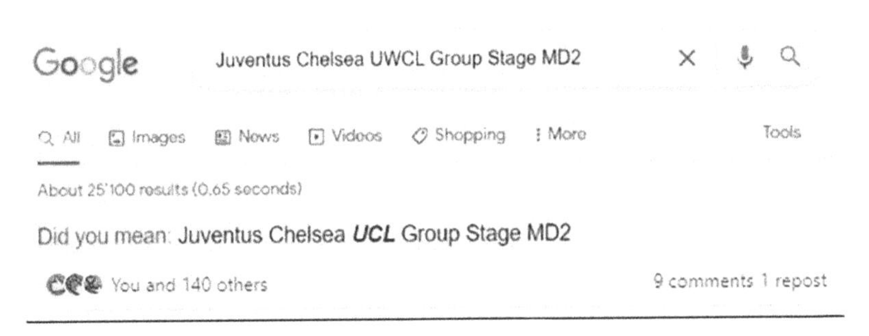

No. Google. I didn't mean that.

Stereotypes Matter

Why is it that when a woman asks to be paid fairly for her experience, challenges an idea or tries to negotiate a pay rise, she is often described as self-important, aggressive or bossy, yet when a man demands his worth, he is quite often labelled as self-assured, assertive and confident, and more often than not he receives yet another promotion? Meanwhile, if a woman questions a decision, or worse, complains, then they are touchy, emotional and feisty.

I guess gender stereotypes have a lot to answer for. Yes, they vary across cultures. However, in the main, men are often linked to words such as dominant, competitive and assertive, whereas women are generally known to be warm, nurturing and passive.

For many women, it's a Catch-22. We are often stuck between a rock and a hard place.

If we want a promotion, we are told and encouraged to show traits that are consistent with powerful leadership stereotypes, which we all know are more often than not associated with masculinity.

Yet, when we act more assertively, we may instantly become less 'likeable' for not being feminine, which in turn limits our chances of climbing the career ladder.

When former New Zealand Prime Minister Jacinda Adern announced her resignation in January 2023, she bravely stated that one of the reasons for her decision was that 'she didn't have enough left in the tank'. And how did the BBC decide to report this story? With a headline which read: 'Can women really have it all?'[6] The headline caused outrage across social media. The BBC apologised. Déjà vu.

Let's be realistic; this woman *really* did have it all. She is a longstanding hero and a world-class, inspirational national leader. Maybe some of those words could have been used in a headline? Maybe? Just saying.

In a 2008 study published in *Psychological Science*, men received a boost in their perceived status after expressing anger. In contrast, 'women who expressed anger were consistently accorded lower status and lower wages and were seen as less competent'.[7]

Another study showed that the perception of women's deserved compensation dropped by 35% (twice as much as men's dropped) when they were equally aggressive in workplace communication. Because likeability can be an even more important factor than competence for getting hired, women who breach gender stereotypes may jeopardise their career prospects.[8]

Media Articles Matter

How about this poignant headline: *'Girls don't like hard maths'*. It was all over the English media in April 2021.

Head teacher Katharine Birbalsingh told members of Parliament that maths was not a subject girls *'tend to fancy'*, adding, *'I just think they don't like it.'*[9]

Kit Yates (a writer for *The Independent*) hit back with this:

'To me, the social mobility tsar Katharine Birbalsingh's supposition about girls not liking hard maths is nothing more than a gender stereotype.'[10]

Masculine or Feminine Matters

In many European languages, objects are either masculine or feminine. In German, the male form is often the default used for plurals, which some argue is sexist and doesn't account for non-binary people.

Head of didactics at Babbel, an online language learning service, warned against confusing gender in grammar with gender in general.

'We have masculine and the feminine—if you would talk about any kind of professional in German, if you use one single word—you have to decide whether you're talking about a male teacher or a female teacher. There is no way in the German language to have it as neutral, as it is in English,' Maren Pauli said.

In October 2022, Cambridge University announced they would stop teaching gendered German, with undergraduates being told to use 'inclusive language' when referring to students or colleagues.

Some linguists hit back saying that native German speakers would think students were speaking foolishly if they didn't use the correct masculine or feminine form.[11]

The debate continues. It's a tough one. Even in English we have words such as policeman, postman, fireman and handyman. Slowly but surely, we are seeing some of these changes, from 'fireman' to 'firefighter', for example. However, humans are creatures of habit, meaning the 'old' labels are still regularly used.

I certainly don't think we can say someone is sexist if they use any of these terms ending in 'man'. These words and phrases have been around for a long time and are naturally part of our vocabulary. But perhaps, these words do matter as it's another example that supports the theory that our world has been designed with men in the front seat and women in the back.

I recently helped a male colleague fix his microphone settings in a teams meeting. His response was "Thanks Sally, you're the man." It was a slip of the tongue and not intentionally sexist, but it is a clear example of a saying which creates a direct association with men and fixing things.

It's Not a Given

There are plenty of examples of women who have broken through the glass ceiling and who are extremely successful. To all of them, I say a huge well done. It is likely they had to work exceptionally hard to get there. There are so many fantastic female role models who all provide hope to young girls today that they too can succeed and break through the stereotypical gender nonsense.

There are also many men who are working wonders as allies in trying to achieve equality. To all of those men out there—thank you. Please keep going and please recruit your friends to follow!

Chapter 3

The Only Way Is Up ... Surely?

2018—Surely Things Will Be Better By Now?

In 2018, I finished working at the Gold Coast Commonwealth Games and started to look for my next adventure. The home of European football in Switzerland, otherwise known as UEFA, was always on my radar.

Three months after applying for a role as online promotion manager and an intense, multiple- stage recruitment process, I finally heard the words that would make working in Switzerland a reality ... 'Congratulations, we would like to inform you, you have been successful!'

After 11-and-a-half years in Australia, it was time to pack up and move to Europe. I was happy, excited, nervous, scared, but ready! Well, I thought I was...

Close friends and family were all happy for me. As the news started to spread, I received countless messages from friends of friends—you know, the ones that hear 'UEFA' and then immediately think *free Champions League final tickets*. The same people who often don't bother to ask how you are, but they would swiftly like to offer their heart-warming congratulations and then, like magic, they will unexpectedly be in touch loads—just coincidentally at the same time their favourite football team is playing in a UEFA competition!

I was not only offered congratulations, but some quite remarkable questions that made me scream with anger ... 'Wow, congratulations on your new job—that's amazing. Who do you know at UEFA? Who did you sleep with? Spill the beans!' Not once, not twice, but three times these types of questions were thrown my way.

Is it not possible for a woman to get a job in football on merit? I didn't even give the questions or the people who asked them the time of day, but they made me furious.

During the recruitment process, I was asked whether I had children and if I had a partner. Apparently, it was so they could work out relocation costs. On arrival at UEFA, I asked male colleagues who were recruited at the same time if they were also asked the same questions during their recent recruitment process—and surprise, surprise, of course they were not. After all, men don't get pregnant.

I received my employment contract along with multiple human resource (HR) policies and the UEFA staff manual—all referenced the employee as a 'he'. Note: this was 2018. Yes, 2018 and the official staff manual referred to all employees as 'he'.

I provided feedback to the HR team and was assured I was not the first person to raise this, and that it would be addressed as soon as possible. I was told it most likely occurred because a non-native English person had created the manual. It was as if that made it okay, and there are no native English speakers at UEFA to check it.

#DiversityAndInclusion

Fast forward to some diversity and inclusion training where we were presented statistics showing the gender split between males and females. 'We are proud that for staff at UEFA, we have a 40% female, 60% male split,' said the presenter, 'but we are not so proud that when we look senior at manager level and above, it is approximately 90% male and 10% female.' Then in the next breath, 'But then again, around 90% of the applications we receive for senior positions are from males, so it's no surprise.'

I raised my hand:

- 'What are you doing to change this?
- What are you doing to attract more females to apply for senior roles?
- What percentage of female staff leave the organisation compared with males?
- Are female staff actively encouraged to apply for senior roles?
- Are you promoting the senior roles on websites where females look?'

'You raise some good points, Sally, and it's something we are looking at closely.'

'Thanks. I hope to see some changes soon as after seeing that graph and realising I am one of the few female managers, I'm a little despondent about my career progression prospects. And perhaps other females are thinking the same?'

I was reminded of the gender split almost daily as I entered meetings, often as the only female. And on some occasions, despite my best efforts (and those who know me will likely back me when I say I have a strong voice), I still couldn't get my voice heard due to the many men dominating the conversation.

February 2019: The Month That Kept on Giving

Remember I said that language matters? It really does. As I mentioned, all the human resource policies I received when I started referred to me as a male. And then only a few months later, an updated travel policy was splashed over the staff intranet and its content made it seem like only men travelled. Just like the HR manual, this must have been written by a non-native English speaker too. Please. Do better.

September 2019: UEFA Interdivisional Staff Tournament

Seven-a-side. The rules: minimum of two girls per team and only one girl needs to be on the field.

Great gender equality message right there.

I excitedly went to collect the kits for our team.

'Here you go, Sally.'

'Thank you. Are there a couple of small, women's kits in there?'

'No, they are all men's kits. We don't have any women's kits.'

This is UEFA, the governing body for 56 international member associations across Europe for men and women. but we don't have any women's kits for a staff competition. No apology. Just fact. Take it or leave it.

It didn't make much sense to me. In one breath, UEFA were actively trying to encourage more female staff to play football—'all abilities are welcome'—and in the next they were giving female staff (who had been repeatedly told to come along and take part, no matter your ability, as football is for everyone) an oversized, ill-fitting men's kit. What a great first impression for all those young women who had never played before.

Then I started to doubt myself. Maybe I was creating a mountain from a molehill. Maybe I was kicking up too much of a fuss. After all, I could definitely play football wearing a men's small kit (despite it still being far too big), but for your information UEFA, a small kit made for female bodies with breasts, hips and waists might have fit me better and made me feel a bit better when I walked out on the pitch. Instead, I was wearing a top that felt like a straight-cut nightdress.

Some teams were given an attractive all-white kit too, because we all know girls on their period love to wear white shorts.

If only a woman had been invited to the table when it came to deciding about the kits, maybe all this could have been avoided. My guess is there were no women involved in the ordering process, and even if there were, their ideas would have likely been shut down.

Football boots and balls are also predominantly designed for men first, women second. And what does this mean? More injuries for women.

Sports scientists are highlighting the lack of football kits designed for women, saying the use of boots and balls created for male players could be putting them at higher risk of injury. Despite some progress, the researchers say no large boot manufacturer has yet invested in a design to suit women.

'Writing in the journal Sport Engineering, a group of sports and exercise researchers, doctors and staff involved in the elite women's game—including England Captain Leah Williamson—point to the need for more kit and technology tailored to women's needs and body shape. For example, football boots fail to account for the fact women's feet, heels and arches are shaped differently.

'And wearing boots designed for men is causing blisters and stress fractures in elite female players. Women also move and run in a different way to men and yet the length of studs on boots are designed around male movement and traction.'[12]

Oh, and remember those uneven, muddy pitches that women are often playing on, quite often cut up from the men the day before—well, hey presto, the same researchers suggested that arrangement increases the risk of injury too:

'Another factor in women's injuries could be playing "on uneven surfaces where men's teams have played the day before."

'Anterior cruciate ligament knee (ACL) injuries are "at least twice as common in elite female footballers when compared to male footballers".'[13]

But It's Not All Bad

In October 2022, West Bromwich Albion decided to change their shorts from white to navy after consultation with female players who raised concerns about having to wear white during their period.

Maybe, just maybe, giving women a seat or two at the decision-making table is a good idea after all.

'West Brom Women will wear navy shorts with their home kit from now on because of concerns about having to wear white while on their periods.

'The players will wear navy for the rest of this season and beyond after discussions with the club.

'Wearing white while on a period is an issue that has been highlighted by women across all sports, including the Lionesses who contacted their kit manufacturer, Nike, after calling their shorts 'not practical' during Euro 2022.

'After consultation with the players, West Brom have taken a forward-thinking approach and confirmed the colour change, with a pledge to consider the situation when designing all future home kits.'

The West Brom captain, Hannah George, told the club website: 'It's great that the club are supporting our change to navy shorts. Representing the club professionally and looking smart in the kit is really important to us. This change will help us to focus on our performance without added concerns or anxiety.'[14]

In October 2022, Manchester City joined the party. They also declared that they would get rid of white shorts for female players from 2023–24.

The same decision was also made for the Lionesses—the England Women's team—for the 2023 World Cup. Progress. Small baby steps. But it's something.[15]

In December 2022, the women's AFL joined the party too!

'Female footballers will no longer have to wear the white shorts traditionally donned by the "away" team after the AFL changed its uniform rules to ease anxiety for AFLW players who are menstruating.

Richmond player Gabby Seymour said players were relieved about the change. '[While white shorts] weren't going to stop anyone from playing, we've got enough things to worry about, so it's nice just to have one extra stressor taken away,' she said.

'We want every female player we can get—so if that's one little thing that we can do that makes girls feel more comfortable to play, then I think that's an awesome outcome.'[16]

It's Ironic, Don't You Think?

In the words of Alanis Morissette, *'It's like ten thousand spoons when all you need is a knife, it's like meeting the man of your dreams and then meeting his beautiful wife'.*

For me, it's like winning a trophy and then being presented with an egg cup! What am I talking about? Read on!

I played football for UEFA Women's FC for a few years. We

trained a couple of times a week at lunchtime and played in a female seven-a-side competition (the Swiss Ligue Romande de Football). In 2021, we won the League.

I didn't go to the awards night, but a few teammates did. They sent a picture of our trophy on a group chat. I had to look twice. Why? Because at first, despite how hard I looked, I could not see it! And then, when I eventually found it (after reaching for the magnifying glass), I couldn't quite believe my eyes. It was lined up next to the other 10 trophies which were ***all*** for men. The women's trophy was by far the smallest on the table; smaller than a half-pint glass and about the size of an egg cup—see the second picture that follows for scale—and it was pink too. Because, didn't you know, all women just *love* pink?

Trophy display table - a bit like where's wally - but this time - where's the minuscule pink trophy?

Miniscule pink trophy next to a half pint size glass for scale.

I might put it next to the award I won at another football club in England. My trophy told me I was 'Club***man*** of the Year'. I know. I'm being harsh; it's not all bad—they did make the trophy figure a woman. One point for effort.

*My club***man** *of the year award from Hassocks Football Club in 2007.*

Did Someone Say Complimentary UEFA Staff Tickets?

I was excited to order my first Champions League staff tickets. I had to log in to the staff ticket portal and complete an application. The system prompted me with a question: *'The requester will attend the match* ***himself****?' Yes, or no?'*

I raised my voice again. It took about four months before it was changed.

November 2019: A Picture Paints a Thousand Words

One day while scanning Twitter, I was greeted with a bold, proud announcement by the Asian Football Confederation (AFC) about their commitment to women's football. The title caught my eye, and then the image made me scream out loud. Yes, I screamed, 'What the actual f%&k?' Followed by something along the lines of: ' ... surely not ... seriously, is this for real? Did someone honestly select this image for this story without a second thought? Are they tone deaf? Stupid? Why is this happening?'

Sadly, I began to realise that as I was seeing things like this so often, my feelings of shock and disbelief had changed to humour—after all, it's better for the soul to laugh rather than cry!

AFC Menu EN | AR

Technical Committee

AFC strengthens commitment to women's football development

Sunday, November 24, 2019

Share on

Tokyo: The Asian Football Confederation's (AFC) continued commitment to women's football in the Continent was underlined by the decision to develop a women's football technical strategy.

The AFC Technical Committee, at their first meeting of the

A picture paints a thousand words

Surely This Will Stop Sometime Soon. It Has To?

At a UEFA Euro 2020 hospitality ticket launch in China in 2019, part of the promotional pitch included young women in crop tops and mini skirts.

I sent a note to a colleague to express my disappointment that this had been allowed in the first instance, and secondly presented in formal presentations to a large number of internal and external stakeholders.

The response?

'Hi Sally, just thought I would let you know that the image has been sent through to the executive office, and the response I got when telling them was that we work very hard in many of our events to not have this happen, so if it has, they want to understand why and if there is anything we can do to ensure it doesn't happen again.'

'***If*** it has?' Clearly it happened. The camera doesn't lie.

Two days later:

'Another update for you! The pictures and situation will be addressed in the next directors' meeting, with the message of why this is not acceptable in any UEFA situation. There will also be some follow-up meetings for further discussions where this is more "likely" to happen. Hopefully this will mean it does not happen again. So, thanks for sharing and let's hope we see no more pictures like that, and if you do come across more, please let me know.'

We all know words can be empty words. Turns out these were empty, meaningless words.

In December 2022, I caught up with a former colleague who had just recently attended the UEFA end-of-year party. I asked how it was. 'It was OK, nothing special,' came the reply.

'Go on, tell me more?' I asked.

'Well, I couldn't quite believe that the entertainment included half-naked pretty girls on stilts strutting up and down corridors with absolutely no purpose whatsoever other than to be glorified objects.'

'Hang on a minute? Half-naked girls?' I asked. 'And were there also half-naked men?' I jokingly replied.

'Don't be silly, of course there were no men! Only women wearing extremely revealing, tight Lycra, pretty much nothing, in fact. I could see everything; as far as I could tell, their sole "purpose" was to parade up and down and occasionally drop in for a photo with staff in Santa's Grotto.'

December 2020—Will This Ever Stop? It Doesn't Look Like It

UEFA proudly launched a four-part documentary series called the *Man in the Middle* about Champions League referees. It was promoted heavily through social media channels, television and e-mails for four weeks. Every day I saw *Man in the Middle* somewhere. Most days, I saw it three to four times. And most of the time it was complemented with a description to encourage me to watch it—*'Find out what it's like to do one of the toughest jobs in football.'* The subliminal message was that only men do the tough jobs.

When I challenged the title and suggested that the name should be changed to portray that thing called 'equality' that we are all supposedly striving towards, I heard every excuse under the sun:

- 'It only features men as its Champions League, so the title is accurate.' This said it all, the response indicated that they had completely ignored the women's Champions League.
- 'Many people challenged the name, including two directors, but it was too late to change.'
- 'Your point is valid, Sally. Many other staff raised it too. But it is too late—the editing has finished.'

Once again, I guess that there were no women involved in the naming of the series. And perhaps, by the time it became known, and women and men politely suggested that it might be a good idea to rethink the title, it was 'too late'. To be fair, many male colleagues agreed with me when I expressed my disappointment, but they too were shot down and told the title was staying. 'The graphics and artwork are done. The budget is over. The edit is final.' And so on.

So every day for four consecutive weeks, I repeatedly read about the *Man in the Middle.*

Then, just a few days later in December 2020, this happened:

Stephanie Frappart becomes first woman to referee in men's Champions League

Oh look. A woman in the middle.[17]

Bravo!

Two years later at the Qatar World Cup, more history was made because for the first time in three women were appointed to officiate a men's match. Brilliant. It's a shame it took so long.

'French referee, Stéphanie Frappart has made history leading the first all-female officiating team for a men's World Cup match, taking charge of Costa Rica v Germany. Frappart is the first woman to referee a men's World Cup match and is joined by the assistant referees Neuza Back of Brazil and Mexico's Karen Díaz Medina for the crucial Group E game.'

Before the tournament began, Frappart said she hoped the inclusion of female referees in Qatar would *'make things happen'* on a broader level. *'It's a strong sign from FIFA and the authorities to have women referees in that country,'* she said.[18]

Next Stop: Moldova, September 2021

My first work trip after the COVID-19 pandemic was to a country I had never travelled to before and knew little about: Moldova. Why? UEFA were hosting a grassroots football festival there and opening a football pitch at a school. I was asked to go to cover the communication, which meant to create content and post various live content pieces on multiple social media channels, write a couple of website stories, source quotes from some VIPs in attendance, and manage the media and the press conferences.

When I was presented with the idea, I was excited and grateful for the opportunity.

Quite swiftly, my travel arrangements arrived in my inbox, and it was then I realised that the whole UEFA Executive Committee were also travelling to Moldova at the same time for a meeting. What did this mean? A private charter plane from Geneva to Moldova. We were asked to arrive at the VIP terminal of Geneva airport. This was new to me! I remember thinking: *VIP terminal? Where is that?* I didn't even know there was such a thing!

Normally I take the train to the airport—do I need to go somewhere else? How do I get there? And then came the list of travellers: me, a few other women, and lots and lots and lots and lots of men. My happiness and excitement were now coupled with anxiety and concern.

I remember being handed my boarding pass on arrival. I took note of the seat number, and thought, *that's at the back of the plane—I'll use the rear door to board.*

And of course, all the very, very important men were seated at the front and the few women were at the back of the aircraft.

To be fair, I don't have a preference and I really couldn't care less where I sit on a plane—I was grateful for the opportunity to travel—but these little hierarchical decisions, whether conscious or unconscious, are little reminders contributing to the ever-growing accumulation of the sexism stepladder.

The grassroots school festival was action-packed and good

fun. After the tiresome COVID lockdowns, it was inspirational and uplifting to see so many young children run around with huge smiles on a brand-new pitch with football superstars. Their eyes lit up from the moment they ran out to the moment they kicked the last ball. The sun shone brightly, and the kids were full of unbounded joy with never-ending smiles and laughter as they effortlessly ran around playing, kicking, screaming and shouting with their friends. It was a pleasant reminder for me about why I love the game so much.

Football is truly amazing. It's such a simple, beautiful game enjoyed by everyone. It brings unity—no matter what a person's age, shape, size or ability may be. It was beautiful to see, especially as we were in one of the poorest European countries in the world where children were often not afforded the simple opportunity of being able to play football at school.

However, it wasn't all smooth sailing. You probably know what's coming next.

It was the last day. I was waiting in the hotel lobby before we boarded the bus to take us to the airport.

A male colleague was standing close to me and said to another male staff member—

Colleague A: 'Sorry I didn't come out last night for long, I was tired after a few too many.'

Colleague B: 'No problem, I wanted to buy you a birthday drink!'

Colleague A: 'Actually, the real reason I didn't come out last night, I was thinking about her (as he pointed in my direction)—she's really hot and beautiful, isn't she?'

I was in shock and said something like, 'Please don't say things like that'—I didn't even know this person (and I hadn't been anywhere but my room and the gym the night before). I found his comment odd, especially as I didn't know him. It was uncomfortable and inappropriate in a work environment. And I was angry.

See-Through. Transparent Trousers Anyone?

I guess when you've been asked to wear your 'transparent' UEFA Euro 2020 uniform trousers to the office so a male senior staff member can check if they really are transparent, I should not be so surprised. And yes, this also happened. For real. In 2021.

For UEFA Euro 2020, the staff uniform included some not-so-lovely beige trousers which were see-through. Understandably, most women decided not to wear them and opted for jeans instead. Smart move. I did the same. However, on my first day wearing the uniform I was asked why I wasn't wearing the trousers—at this point, I didn't know they were transparent—I had just seen everyone wearing jeans, so I followed suit. I said, 'Well, it seems like hardly anyone is wearing them, so I chose jeans!'

'Well, maybe you can wear them tomorrow, Sally, so I can check?'

It wasn't until I got home that night and relived the conversation in my head that I thought, *what the actual F*!K?* I should have called him out or at least reported the conversation to Human Resources. Instead, I nervously laughed and moved the conversation on as quickly as possible. Why? Because I was tired. Tired of the same old nonsense. These things were happening so regularly.

A colleague told me about another scenario from a Euro 2020 debrief workshop where there was a positive statement made by a male senior staff member: 'Despite the global pandemic, the revenue generated from concessions almost equalled 2016, so we can be really happy and proud. A big well done to everyone. And what helped us achieve this? We sold beer.

'So, for Euro 2024, let's write down two must-haves—alcohol and women—then it will be the best party ever.'

Talking of 2024—there were some bold statements aligned with the brand when it launched—'Football is for everyone. Diversity and inclusion—this is what the logo is all about—football is a home for all.'

So, let's look at the invited guests to the brand launch in Germany ... 40 men and two women. Let's look at the speakers at the event.

All men. OK then. Football is for everyone.

March 2020. Hello COVID-19. Hello, Working From Home. Hello Virtual Backgrounds

Sally's personalised virtual Teams background

Why did I make my own virtual background when working from home?

I did it as a statement. Unsurprisingly, all of the virtual backgrounds sent to us by UEFA featured men only. I remember getting all excited when the email dropped—oh look, we have some new virtual backgrounds to use (crazy how these small things were sometimes the biggest things happening during the lockdown days).

With my kitchen table doubling as my office, a new virtual background that could hide the mess was semi-exciting! My sense of enthusiasm didn't last long. There were four or five images—and as I flicked from one to the next hoping to see a female, I was instead just met with more white men and then some more and then some more, yes, white men.

Once again, I raised it and my comments were heard—'Yes, Sally, another really good point—you are not the first to write to me. We will make sure the next set features women.' I felt like I was being labelled as 'the annoying one'—*'Yes. Yes, Sally. Here you go again.*

Please be quiet. We know, because loads of other staff said the same. Please do be quiet now.'

A few months passed and a few more virtual backgrounds were rolled out. Despite being told that the next set would feature women, set two also only featured lovely white men. My feedback was pointless. I'm sure the other staff who wrote similar emails to me were also 'happy' to see their thoughts and suggestions ignored.

When you consider approximately seven hundred staff would be using these virtual backgrounds daily with a variety of internal and external stakeholders present during online meetings; maybe, just maybe, it would have been wise to use this as an opportunity to promote 'equality'.

March 8, 2021

March 8 each year is International Women's Day. What does that even mean? I remember reading more than ever about it on this particular day in 2021. It was all over my newsfeeds and also on the television and radio.

But what is it?

It's a United Nations-backed day.

'Advancing gender equality in the context of the climate crisis and disaster risk reduction is one of the greatest global challenges of the 21st century.

Women are increasingly being recognized as more vulnerable to climate change impacts than men, as they constitute the majority of the world's poor and are more dependent on the natural resources which climate change threatens the most.

At the same time, women and girls are effective and powerful leaders and change-makers for climate adaptation and mitigation. They are involved in sustainability initiatives around the world, and their participation and leadership results in more effective climate action.

Continuing to examine the opportunities, as well as the constraints, to empower women and girls to have a voice and be equal players in decision-making related to climate change and sustainability is essential for sustainable development and greater gender equality.

Without gender equality today, a sustainable future, and an equal future, remains beyond our reach.

This International Women's Day, let's claim "Gender equality today for a sustainable tomorrow"'.[19]

I decided to jump on the bandwagon and write a post on LinkedIn to tell my story and also vent my frustration. I was slowly learning to be brave and to speak up without being afraid of any potential backlash.

LinkedIn Post: March 2021

'As a young girl, I loved football and I wanted to play like the boys.

Yet, at the age of seven when I asked my PE teacher if I could play football with the boys, I was told firmly:

No, Sally. Football is for ***boys,*** *Sally. You can play hockey or netball.*

If I had listened and I didn't #ChooseToChallenge, I would not have achieved:

The only full academic scholarship to study a Master of Business specialising in Sport Management at Griffith University, in 2007.

My research focused on increasing female participation rates in football in Australia.

I have worked in professional football since 2015, for Football Federation Australia, the AFC Asian Cup 2015, Melbourne City FC, Wellington Phoenix FC, Brisbane Roar FC, UEFA and the UEFA Foundation for Children.

I coached Under 16 boys' football at the University of Queensland. We finished second.

I have had over 50 articles published as a paid freelance football writer covering a range of topics including but not limited to Brighton and Hove Albion FC, the A-League, the Premier League, UEFA Euro 2016, the UEFA Champions League, fan engagement and marketing.

I have interviewed Premier League footballers and world-famous international football players.

I have presented to all UEFA staff.

I have presented at an official board meeting for the UEFA Foundation to the UEFA President.

After being told no several times, I ensured 10 fans attended the UEFA Euro final draw in 2019 in Bucharest. I #ChoseToChallenge which meant fans experienced the final draw for the **first time** *in UEFA's history.*

I have been a guest panellist on a Sports Pro Insider webinar about communication and marketing football.

I played football and futsal for almost 20 years.

Imagine if I had listened to my PE teacher and I didn't #ChooseToChallenge?

Football is for EVERYONE. Don't let anyone tell you differently.

Don't get me wrong, working in a male-dominated world is far from easy, but it's possible. And although writing this post is taking me out of my humble personality, perhaps it's important to shout loudly about our achievements, just like men do.

Why?

We need to ensure children growing up do not have the same biases that many people carry today. And if I can be a role model to just one young girl who is trying to work in football, this post is worthwhile.

So often when I talk, it is assumed I know nothing about football, just because I am a woman.

But you know what? I love picking my moment and watching the jaws drop of men as they realise that actually not only do I know what I am talking about, but sometimes I know **more** *than them.*

We shouldn't need to fight this hard to be respected. It is tiring and exhausting fighting these daily battles. So, let's say it again ...

Football is for **everyone.** *Don't let anyone tell you differently.'*[20]

February 2022

I was in an online communication workshop. We were assigned a group task—

Task: Brainstorm how UEFA can promote and celebrate an art exhibition at UEFA Headquarters which will showcase sixteen female artists from each of the host nations for Women's Euro.

Male colleague A: 'There is no such thing as a female artist—how ridiculous, I hope these women haven't been asked to contribute just because they are women. Why are there no paintings from men? We don't need to say female artist, we need to just say artist. Look at French politics, x y and z have held their respective positions for x years only because they are women. It's a joke. Similarly, there is no such thing as women's literature. It's just literature.' And so he went on and on and on and on.

I was shocked. I replied:

'The reason we should celebrate and promote female artists is because they most likely haven't been afforded the same opportunities as male artists, not to mention the backdrop of gender inequality we have seen in the last 50 years. And wait, let me check—for men's Euro, you know, the Euro we never refer to as *men's* Euro, just Euro—we had an exhibition of 32 paintings—and guess what—all the artists were male. Funny that. Following your logic, I guess we should call Women's Euro, "Euro". But wait, that's associated with men. So, we do need to call it Women's Euro. Oh, and only a few months ago UEFA was celebrating and promoting the toughest job in football, also known as a referee, with a documentary titled *The Man in the Middle*.'

'Your examples are relevant, and you raise a valid point about inclusion in general, but welcome to our world—for every single example you have, I have several hundred to counter your point,' I said.

Several colleagues (male and female) tried to support me and raised other valid points:

'You are completely ignoring the historical context of inequality and how it's embedded in our modern mentality and consciousness.'

But to my astonishment, that wasn't enough ... and colleague A piped up again, rambling some more about how the task was pointless and that we should never celebrate female artists.

The conversation went on for so long that we had hardly any time to focus on the meeting task itself.

Conclusion: dinosaurs will be dinosaurs.

On a recent trip to Gatwick Airport, I popped into a well-known bookstore. The main display on entry caught my eye. Why? It was celebrating women's writing. I thought of colleague A as I took a picture and that he would likely tell me that female authors don't need celebrating.

Celebrating women's writing

April 4, 2022: South America and Europe Unite

Let's play a game. Do you see what I see? There is one woman in the following picture (look carefully). Found her? Yes. Me too. She's the one with half her face cut off. Quite symbolic really, don't you think? So, what was the picture for? To promote a news story about a shared office between CONMEBOL and UEFA.

Through the agreement, UEFA and CONMEBOL will look to organise a variety of football events, while also cooperating in other areas such as refereeing and coaching programs.

Lots of men in suits.

What Is Finalissima?

The 2022 Finalissima (Italian for 'grand final'; Spanish: 'finalísima') was the third edition of the CONMEBOL–UEFA Cup of Champions, an intercontinental football match between the winners of the previous South American and European championships. It featured Italy, winners of UEFA Euro 2020 (held in 2021 due to COVID), and Argentina, winners of the 2021 Copa América, and was played at Wembley Stadium in London, England, on June 1, 2022. The match, a revival of the Artemio Franchi Cup last played 29 years prior, was organised by UEFA and CONMEBOL as part of a renewed partnership between the two confederations.

Argentina won the match 3–0 for their second CONMEBOL–UEFA Cup of Champions title.[21]

But wait a minute. Is there a female version too? Of course there is. It even has its own Wikipedia page but guess what ... it's called ***women's*** Finalissima and the first one will happen in 2023. That makes sense. We need to let the men get the exclusive naming rights and go first. Silly me.[22]

Some light at the end of the tunnel. But it's not all bad, I promise. Eventually, I said, enough is enough. Let's stop whingeing and attempt to make some changes.

In April 2022, I initiated a staff working group at UEFA called 'Together for Equality'. It wasn't easy to get going, and ironically involved getting sign-off from a lot of senior male staff, but it was a baby step in the right direction. As I seemed to have little or no power in being able to bring about change, I thought collective power might be a better strategy; I wanted to make an informal working group of UEFA staff who would work collaboratively to generate innovative ideas to improve gender equality.

I became aware that there had already been a few informal meetings organised between a few female staff and the Human Resources department about this exact topic prior to the COVID-19 pandemic, but nothing had been formalised and the group meetings lost momentum when we went into lockdown.

I approached HR with my idea and after a few meetings and some lengthy emails to every *man* and his dog, the idea was eventually approved. I was given permission to publish a story on the staff intranet. The main objectives of the group were:

- To formulate ideas which would raise awareness, educate, and shape attitudes around gender equality at UEFA.
- To implement initiatives which would directly improve gender equality at UEFA—for example, by improving gender balance at managerial level and above, enhancing gender diversity on UEFA-organised panels (webinars, presentations, press conferences, etc.) and advancing gender balance across part-time roles.

It was a mini breakthrough. I was so determined because inequality, especially in senior management positions at UEFA, was shocking.

In April 2022, employee statistics showed there were 714 staff at UEFA; 435 (60%) were male and 279 (40%) were female. That's not too bad. But let's look a bit closer:

- There were 32 staff at chief-to-president-level; 30 were male (93%) and two were female (7%).
- At manager-to-head of level (so slightly less senior), the picture

wasn't much better—there were 315 staff; 232 were male (74%) and 83 were female (26%).

- But when we looked at the bottom end of the hierarchy ... At apprentice-to-team lead level, there were 367 staff; 173 were male (47%) and 194 were female (53%).

So, somewhere, something was going wrong! The data shows that as you progress through the ranks (particularly at manager level and above) of this organisation, there are significantly less women than men, despite there being almost parity at the lower levels.

Why Does This Matter?

Women and girls represent half of the world's population and therefore also half of its potential, yet on average, less than one in three senior and middle management positions are held by women.[23]

- Everyone benefits from gender equality; societies that value women and men as equal are safer and healthier.

Gender equality has been shown to improve profitability and the overall performance of companies. The business case for diversity in teams is strong, particularly in executive teams as numerous studies have demonstrated, including McKinsey's 2020 analysis.[24]

The study showed that companies in the top quartile for gender diversity on executive teams were 25% more likely to have above-average profitability. And lastly, companies with more than 30% women executives were more likely to outperform companies where this percentage ranged from 10 to 30.

Positively, UEFA were trying to address the imbalance and during the period I was there, there were a number of initiatives implemented to try and create constructive change.

Examples included a new parental leave policy, an inclusive language guide, equal pay certification, a women in leadership program run by the UEFA Academy, an internal staff newsletter on women's football, and a staff survey around diversity and inclusion.

In the first working group meeting I attended, we also discussed some new ideas:

- A mentoring program.
- Advertising senior UEFA roles on websites that are targeted at women.
- An inclusive language guide for oral communication.
- Inclusive imagery around UEFA headquarters (HQ)—as an example, for the four years I was there, the history of football that you see on entry into UEFA headquarters features only men's football.
- Renaming UEFA meeting rooms (in the time I was there, all meeting rooms were named after men).
- More gender diversity at official UEFA events (webinars, panels, presentations, press conferences).
- Diversity and inclusion training and refresher courses for all staff.
- An increase in the number of women's matches on the UEFA staff predictor game. I played this game online every week for a few years, as did hundreds of other staff. Each week, we were invited to guess the result (i.e., highlight the winning team or predict a draw for approximately 20 men's games and one women's game per week). Naturally, the *one* women's game was highlighted in a different colour to make sure users knew this game was 'different' than the others. But by changing its colour, it also quickly showed that the one women's game was the odd one out.

Of course, I brought it up. 'But Sally, there are less European female games than male games each weekend, so of course there are more men's matches in our predictor game.'

'Yes. That is true. But I'm also quite sure that if you could find one women's match to include in the game, then you could definitely find a few more.'

Chapter 4

Dreams Do Come True

England were in a European final in my lifetime. I couldn't quite believe it.

UEFA Euro 2020 Final England vs Italy July 11,2021

Wembley Stadium, London

A day and night to remember, and to forget.

Where to start?

About 10 days before the UEFA Euro 2020 final, UEFA sent an email to all staff outlining ticket allocations. It explained that staff were going to be offered two complimentary tickets to the final, but if any staff member decided to travel, they would need to follow all associated rules linked to COVID-19 quarantine and tests.

At this point, England had beaten Ukraine in the quarter-final and were facing Denmark in the semi-final. To go or not to go, that was the question on my mind.

To go home would mean extortionate, overpriced flights, six days of strict quarantine and multiple rip-off (i.e. likely non-functional) COVID-19 tests. VIPs, by the way, were granted an exception to these rules. Why? Because it's one rule for them and one rule for us. Staff joked that COVID-19 must be so clever, it could tell the difference between a VIP and a 'normal' person. Wow!

Decisions, decisions. On the one hand, there was no guarantee England would be in the final, so it was a big risk, especially with the added COVID-19 related expenses and quarantine—but on the other hand, England were only one match away from making their first major final in 55 years. If England made it and I didn't go, I would be kicking myself. What a dilemma to face! Sometimes we need a little reminder that life is short, and once I had that little nugget of wisdom, I decided to go for it. Worst case, England would lose the semi-final and I'd still experience the Euro final at Wembley. It's really not a bad worst-case scenario.

So, some expensive flights and three COVID-19 tests later, I made it to England. A couple of days later, England were playing in the semi-final against Denmark.

England won. And breathe... It was also the start of my personal World War III. Why? Because this also meant I had to decide who to take as my plus one!

After much deliberation, I decided to take my brother, who (believe it or not), doesn't really like or follow football, but I was sure he would still enjoy the occasion.

The hype around the match was enormous. Non-stop media coverage. It presented itself as the perfect timely opportunity for fans to go all out. To go wild. It was a 'perfect storm' scenario. People were rightly or wrongly likely to go crazy as they released all the negative emotions they had been experiencing over the last couple of years. Watch out—caged animals were about to be unleashed, en masse!

Sunday July 11, 2021, arrived. I was like a kid in a candy store. So excited. I woke up at the crack of dawn and I couldn't wait to start our journey to London. We boarded the train from Hove to London Victoria station around 10 o'clock. From there, we took the tube to the Park Royal where we were staying. On arrival at our hotel, we were greeted by many loud, brash England fans who were in full voice and already had enough beers lined up for an army! As we waited to check in, I noticed the televisions were showing live coverage from Wembley. To my surprise, it was already packed and looking a little messy and disordered (some eight hours before kick-off!). I even said to the receptionist, 'They are not live pictures, are they? It can't be that busy already there? The images must be from the semi-final a couple of days ago.'

'No—this is definitely live,' she said. 'That's Wembley Way right now.'

Wow. I started to feel excited and said to my brother, 'We should get ready now and head there already—looks like lots of fun!' We did exactly that—checked in, grabbed some lunch and then set off to Wembley Stadium.

On arrival at Wembley Central tube station, the noise, colour and atmosphere were electric. England fans were singing loudly and proudly and most appeared in good spirits. I was a little shocked about how many fans already seemed 'out of it', and also at the giant piles of endless litter which greeted us (Wembley Way was already covered with bottles, beer cans and clutter, so much so that you couldn't see the pavement). As I walked through the crowds, I found myself wedged in my own tracks as my feet often got stuck firmly to the surface like it had the strongest superglue known to man. Gross.

Despite the stickiness, we soaked up the atmosphere and started to embrace the surroundings. But within an hour or two, it was clear that in some areas, it was beginning to get out of control. There were fans climbing and walking on roofs, climbing and swinging from traffic lights and lamp posts, throwing bottles, street cones, leather footballs and more.

As the afternoon advanced, the gluey floor became even worse as men to the left, to the right and some even in the centre decided to use it as a toilet. How lovely. I remember wanting to get out of the middle of the crowd as it was too chaotic and 'sticky'. I said to my brother, 'Let's go to the edge—it's too crazy here.' I had just seen a policeman with his face covered in blood.

We scrambled our way to the edge ... and I thought, *phew, that feels better.* And just as I thought we had escaped the madness, I looked up to see a crowd of men all taking a piss against a wall in full view of everyone. How lovely.

I had such a choice to make. I could stand in the middle and risk maybe getting a glass bottle thrown at my head, or I could escape to the edge where I could at least breathe and move freely, but I also might get pissed on.

Despite these few moments of feeling unsafe, in general I was going with the flow and having fun. On one occasion, a random young

England fan appeared out of nowhere and decided to embrace me. He put his arms around my waist and kissed me on the cheek without a care in the world. He said something like 'Look after your wife, she's gorgeous' to my brother and asked for a picture. Harmless? Maybe. But still not right. Why do men think this is okay? For the record, it's not okay to approach a woman that you don't know, put your arm around her and then kiss her. My brother said something like 'She's my sister, not my wife' ... He didn't seem to care—like many fans, he was extraordinarily drunk.

Before this encounter, I caught an inflatable beach ball that was being passed around the crowds. I was about to kick it high in the air when a guy next to me tried to grab it out of my hands and said, 'Can I kick it?'

'No. I caught it!'

'But you're a girl.'

And with that I smashed the ball (almost into smithereens) high, high above the crowds.

'Wow. You kicked that better than me,' he said.

'No shit, Sherlock. Girls can play football too. And by the way, beach balls aren't the only balls I can kick.'

And that was the end of that conversation. Sally 1, sexist random fan 0.

About two hours before kick-off, around six o'clock, we decided to head into the stadium.

The first thing that should have been checked was our negative COVID test or proof of full vaccine via the National Health Service (NHS) application. Lots of fans were struggling to get their NHS app to work as the internet wasn't working—probably due to the volume of people in the area. My brother and I were ushered through with no check whatsoever—a quick glance, if that, and we were through checkpoint one.

Admittedly, the stewards had an extremely difficult job—it almost felt like it was safer to let everyone pass through without any checks than it was to stop people. Why? Because the crowds were rapidly building along Wembley Way which was beginning to feel dangerous; bottlenecks started to form and people began to get irate, frustrated and impatient—some fans were pushing their way through with extreme force.

Once inside the stadium perimeter, we used our mobile tickets to enter which was a smooth process. We took some time to browse the official merchandise and then made our way to the concourse near our seats. Fans were in full voice once again, mainly singing the infamous 'Please don't take me home' song repeatedly. I saw drugs being exchanged. I saw excessive drinking everywhere. I said to my brother, 'If England wins tonight, I'm not sure we will get home safely.'

The chaos was beginning to feel senseless, out of control and insane, and this was before the match. I had never seen pandemonium quite like it and I have seen football all around the world. During the last hour before kick-off, I started to get concerned about safety. As kick-off neared, it got worse.

About 40 minutes before kick-off, mainly to escape the chaos on the concourse, we decided to head to our seats. Bizarrely, there were people already sitting in them—two young boys. When I asked them to move, they jumped up with no problem. I thought it was a bit strange, but at this time, I had no clue about the developing situation outside the stadium that would explain why there were random people sitting in our seats: several thousand ticketless fans had broken into the stadium by various means—through gates for people with a disability and by breaking down huge barriers.

As the match kicked off, there were many fans sitting on the stairwell right next to me. I was naturally concerned as anyone who works in sport events knows that stairwells must be kept clear at all times in case there is a need to evacuate. Even more worrying was that despite multiple fans complaining, stewards did not seem to care one single bit. After about 15 minutes, all the fans who were sitting in the stairwell were eventually, albeit timidly, requested to move. A few moved. The majority stayed. The stewards appeared powerless.

As for the match itself, we don't need to go there! For those who don't recall it, here's a quick summary.

Despite England taking an early lead, Italy equalised. The match went to extra time and England lost on penalties. Cue: more ghastly, horrible discrimination and disorder.

'Fan disorder which marred the Euro 2020 final at Wembley was a "near miss" of fatalities and a "source of national shame", an independent review commissioned by the Football Association has found.

'The review carried out by Baroness Louise Casey of Blackstock found that approximately 2,000 ticketless fans gained entry to the stadium, of which around 400 were ejected, for the showpiece between England and Italy on July 11.

'Bullingham added: "Collectively we must never allow this to happen again. Baroness Casey is clear that moving forwards, where there is an event of national significance, we and all agencies must view it through a different lens."'[25]

As shocking as it was, I was hopeful that it would raise alarm bells and action would be taken to ensure nothing like that ever happens again.

After attending the final, I was invited to talk on a *Women in Football Australia* podcast about my experiences attending the final as a fan. It turns out others experienced it too.

When Bristol Rovers fans Lucy Ford and Caz May began speaking to other female football fans, they quickly realised the abuse they had experienced both online and in person (for simply being women who like football) was a much more widespread issue.

It is why the duo, along with 10 other female football supporters, decided to launch the 'Her Game Too' campaign to combat sexism within the sport.

The message they are promoting is a simple one: to foster a positive, inclusive environment in football, while raising awareness and educating others about the abuse women who follow football regularly face.

Now, the Her Game Too message is being backed by clubs such as Swansea City, Exeter City, Tranmere Rovers, Newport County, Yeovil Town and Grimsby Town, as well as May and Ford's own team, Bristol Rovers.

'That's really what it's about, it's about inspiring the next generation of female football fans, female footballers,' Ford said. 'And just saying that, you know, you should be allowed to be a female football fan, a female footballer, without being told that you shouldn't because you're a female.'[26]

And guess what else? In a fantastic, emotional, piece written by Caoimhe O'Neill in July 2021, she powerfully articulated what it's like to be a woman watching the men's England team. Almost every single word resonated with my own experience. The headline says it all:

This is what you endure watching England as a woman: Misogyny, sexism and the constant fear of being touched without consent[27]

In September 2021, the men's head coach, Gareth Southgate said:

'There are not enough women in the England men's national team set-up. More work needs to be done to increase the number of women in the England men's senior team backroom staff.'

Southgate named two women who are currently working with the team:

'*We've got a staff of 40, so that's nowhere near where we should be.'*

He pointed out that the picture, in terms of gender equality, is better across the whole of the Football Association but still thinks there is room for improvement. He said:

'Within the FA we are actually very diverse, gender-wise, with 38 percent female, I think. 'But as my daughter said to me, "Oh, that's good is it, Dad?" I had to say, "Er, good point."'[28]

I am extremely happy that I got to experience a match of a lifetime. There were some magical moments that will stay with me forever, such as the red arrows flying over Wembley just before kick-off, the extraordinary, deafening roar after England scored in the third minute, and seeing so many fans, young and old, enjoy themselves after two incredibly hard corona-fuelled years. They are the huge moments that spring to mind. My Instagram post from the day after the big day sums up my elation:

UEFA Euro 2020 final

About last night. I don't have the words, but I'll try!

An exciting, thrilling, nail-biting emotional rollercoaster which was off-the-scale pandemonium.

An atmosphere like I've never, ever experienced in my life.

Some incredible memories for the bank.

More photos and videos to follow once I've been through the 500 on my phone!

60,000 English fans going absolutely mental for 120 minutes … unique, memorable and very, very special.

It's not coming home, but wow.

Well played, England football team. You can be very, very, very proud.

Well done, Italy. To win the final away from home with 60,000 English fans and only 7,000 Italian fans ... just wow.

Thank you UEFA for making a dream come true for me. There were many bumps over the last three years, but we got there.

51 matches in 11 countries. Done.

1.5 million tickets sold.

I certainly 'Lived It. For Real' last night and despite the result, I'm still smiling.

But miserably, with the benefit of hindsight, the significant, extraordinary lows outweighed the highs; the never-ending chaos, the constant disorder, the endless foolishness, the visible drugs, the overflowing drinks, the flying glass bottles, the absurd sexist comments—the unleashed caged animals really did go for it; they were set free and went all out—wild and senseless.

I was so glad that I decided not to take my mum. I would have spent the whole day fearing for her safety. And I am extremely grateful that I didn't get caught up in the major disorder and chaos that unfolded outside before kick-off.

As Baroness Casey's independent report noted, we were incredibly lucky that no one lost their lives. Ironically, had England won on the night, I think we may well have experienced a tragedy.

Chapter 5

Newsfeeds and Sexism

Whilst writing this book, I sent myself website links to sexism stories that I stumbled across when browsing world media. And guess what? The 'To Sally, From Sally' message thread comprises *hundreds and hundreds* of links.

Below is a selection for a rather tantalising sexism storyboard. I've picked a few of my favourites.

Gold Medal—German FA

In first place, in March 2021, the story of Heiko Vogel, coach of Borussia Monchengladbach's Under-23 men's side. Vogel was suspended for two matches, fined approximately $1,800, and commanded to coach the women's team for six sessions as ***punishment*** for 'unsporting behaviour' towards officials during a game in January. Yes, you read that right.

So, coaching women is a 'punishment'?

Let's apply the same logic to another situation: Let's imagine a female coach committed 'unsporting behaviour' towards match officials. OK. And now let's envision her punishment as coaching six sessions for the men's team? Sounds ridiculous that way around, doesn't it?

The intention might have been positive—perhaps it was thought that an experienced coach would give something back to the grassroots of the sport by coaching women. However, it is appalling to imply that coaching a female team is a form of penalty for a manager. Women's football is a sport; those who participate in it are as professional as their male counterparts.[29]

Silver Medal—Irish Rugby

In August 2020, a leading sports manufacturer came under fire for using models instead of current players to launch the new Ireland women's national team rugby jersey. Why? I guess, because someone—perhaps a man or maybe some men—decided that the real players are not 'beautiful' enough.

Unsurprisingly, manufacturer Canterbury issued an apology after social media went into a frenzy with fans commenting on how disappointed they were with the decision.

RUGBY UNION

'Female players don't look good enough to sell kits? Well, politely, look at Lionel Messi . . .'

Elgan Alderman speaks with Victoria Rush about a new film exposing the casual sexism putting some women off rugby

Ireland used models instead of their own rugby players for the women's kit launch in 2020

The journey towards making a film about the status of women's rugby started for Victoria Rush when Canterbury launched Ireland's kit in 2020 using models. The men's apparel was worn by players, famous and with the potential for further growth in profile; the women's was superimposed on to people who do not play the sport.

Models instead of players. Ouch.

The following tweet says it all:

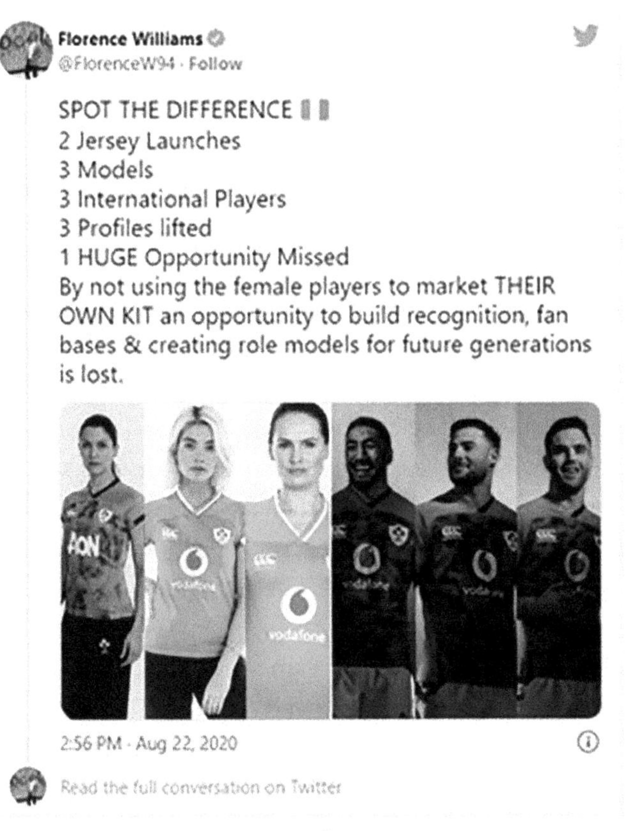

Spot the difference.[30]

In September 2022, England and the Rugby Football Union were busy defending their decision to fly favourites England to the women's Rugby World Cup in New Zealand in economy class, in stark contrast to their male counterparts who flew business class to Japan in 2019 for the (men's) Rugby World Cup.

While there is an argument that women's teams are not always as profitable as a men's team—it's a bit blah blah. It was 2022. When will we invest smartly so women have the best chance to become profitable? If you are aiming to provide your professional players, also known as elite athletes, with the best chance of winning the biggest tournament in the world rugby calendar, then squishing the team into economy class seats for a journey from one side of the world to the other for over 30 hours might not be the greatest plan?[31]

Bronze Medal: Graeme Souness, August 2022

The English Premier League was back after the summer break, and back it came with a big bang in a scintillating match between Chelsea and Arsenal that ended in a 2–2 draw.

After the match, Graeme Souness (a Scottish former professional football player and manager, and pundit on Sky Sports) exclaimed live on television that he had loved watching the drama of a thrilling draw between Chelsea and Arsenal football because:

'It's a man's game all of a sudden again. I think we've got our football back, as I would enjoy football—men at it, blow for blow, and the referee letting them get on with it.'

Cue uproar. Some people said, 'So what?' He was talking about men's football, so what was the problem? Some women disagreed—hang on a minute, did you not just see what happened only two weeks previously? In case you missed it, the England **women's** team were crowned European champions.

Football is not just a man's game—it's for everyone. And you know what, the women who received those gold medals are strong, brave and fierce, and they went one step further than the men the year before.

Bethany England wasn't having any of it.[32]

When given the chance to explain his comments, Souness emphasised he was also giving praise to the referees, referencing his love for their free-flowing style that was a pleasant contrast to the whistle-happy, stop-start style which had been the dominant pattern of recent seasons.

However, I do think he could perhaps have chosen his words more wisely. Why? Because what he said could easily be misconstrued and some will likely have interpreted it to mean something along the lines of, *'Let's get back to aggressive football. Men fighting on the pitch and off it. That's how it should be. That's how I like it. That's how I remember it.'* And to some, that could suggest that women are not welcome yet again—because let's not forget, women were banned from playing football in England in 1921 for 50 years.

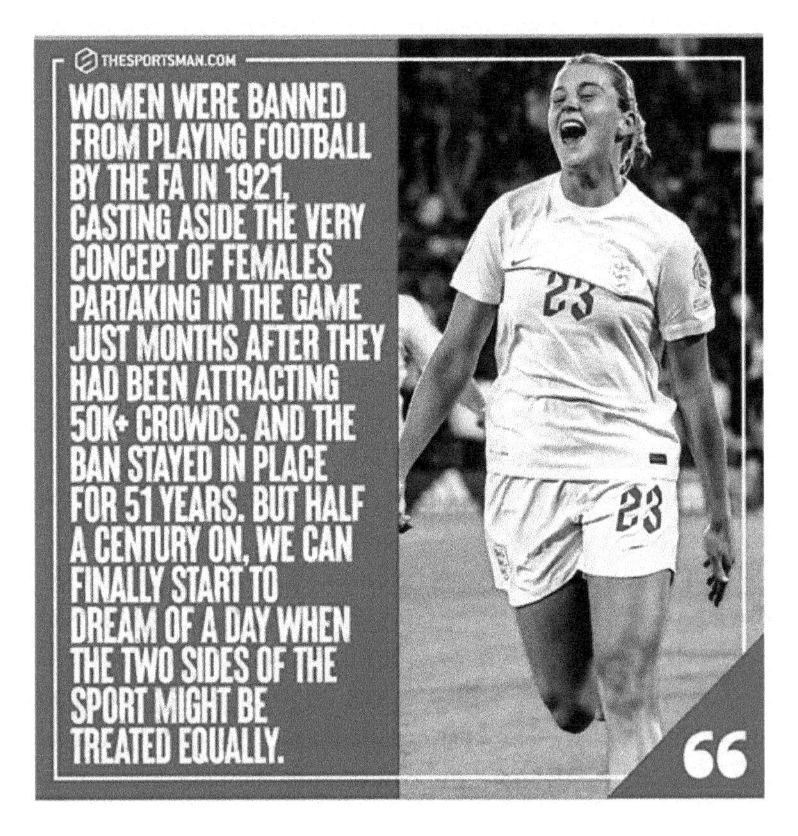

Yes, you read that right. Women were banned from playing football for fifty years.

Despite women having been thrown out of workplaces in large numbers and the return of men's football after its suspension between 1915 and 1919 in the United Kingdom (because of World War I), the women's game was flourishing at the turn of the 1920s, with the Dick, Kerr Ladies FC—a team from Preston—leading the way.

In 1920, Dick, Kerr Ladies played four international home fixtures against a French team led by women's sport activist, Alice Milliat, at Deepdale, Stockport, in Manchester and then Stamford Bridge. The team then went to France and played in Paris, Roubaix, Le Havre and Rouen. It would prove to be a hugely popular tour and on the team's return to England, the hype for a scheduled Boxing Day match against rivals St Helens at Goodison Park was building. Few though could have predicted the seismic impact the fixture would have on the future of women's football.

On the day of the match, 53,000 fans filed into the ground for the game and according to the diary of player, Alice Stanley, a further 10–15,000 supporters were turned away.

It reportedly broke another record too, with the *Lancashire Evening Post* on December 28, 1920, saying:

'The most remarkable "gate" of the holiday, however, was at Goodison Park yesterday morning [Boxing Day] where the Dick, Kerr Ladies beat St Helens Ladies 4–0 in a match on behalf of the unemployed and disabled ex-servicemen. The attendance was estimated at 53,000 and the receipts were over £3,000 exclusive of tickets. This being an easy record for a charity match in England.'

And then promptly afterwards, the devastation of the women's game came at lightning speed.

The English Football Association (the FA) were not blind to the growing popularity and success of women's football. The huge sums of money being raised were outside their jurisdiction and control.

So, one year after more than 53,000 fans watched on at Goodison Park, the FA voted to ban women's football! The sport's governing body did not have the power to ban women from playing outright—that was impossible, so instead they ruled that women's games were barred from FA-affiliated football grounds.

Astonishingly, the ban lasted a gruelling 51 years.

Why? The ruling stated this:

'Complaints having been made as to football being played by women, Council felt impelled to express the strong opinion that the game of football is quite unsuitable for females and should not be encouraged. Complaints have also been made as to the conditions under which some of the matches have been arranged and played, and the appropriation of receipts to other than charitable objects. The Council are further of the opinion that an excessive proportion of the receipts are absorbed in expenses and an inadequate percentage devoted to charitable objects.

'For these reasons the Council requests the Clubs belonging to the Association refuse the use of their grounds for such matches.'

The Dick, Kerr Ladies' Captain, Alice Kell, described in the press as an 'unassuming, intelligent working girl,' said:

'We girls play football in a proper spirit. We do not retaliate if we are bowled over, and we show no fits of temper. We are all simply amazed at the action of the authorities in placing a ban upon the sport we love with all our heart. Surely to goodness we have the right to play any game we think fit without interference from the Football Association! We are all working girl's dependent upon our weekly wages and living with our parents and others partly dependent upon us.'

When I mention this important slice of history to people, they find it hard to believe. Many ask why the women didn't continue playing football outside FA stadiums.

The fact is it was hard to attract big crowds when the teams were forced to play at local parks, small rugby or athletics clubs. The huge stadiums offered to men's football clubs could not be matched. And so, without the opportunity to entice big crowds at large-capacity venues, the interest in women's football naturally declined.[33]

And the Rest

In June 2022, French Open tennis director, Amelie Mauresmo, apologised for saying women's matches were less appealing than men's and said she had been quoted *"out of context"*.

She faced criticism after only one of the new night sessions for the 2022 event featured a women's match, and apologised for

"The people who know me, who've known me on and off the court, throughout my career, throughout everything that I've done, know I'm a big fighter for equal rights and women's tennis, women in general."[34]

Maybe Mauresmo's words were slightly twisted by the media and blown up to be something bigger than their original meaning, but even so, this story ignited a fierce debate. Are men's matches really more appealing? If so, why? And if tennis is striving for equality, perhaps there should be some consideration towards broadcasting more women's matches during prime-time television?

We need to strive for equality not equity. There is a big difference.

But even when men and women share the same stage across the same time frame, as they do at the four tennis grand slams across the world (which in itself portrays a big step towards equity compared to a lot of other sports), there is still room for sexism.

A Little Anecdote from Positano, Italy

In November 2022, I took a taxi from Positano on the Amalfi Coast in Italy to Naples Airport. With a journey the length of a football match ahead of us, and given we were in a country where residents adore football more than most, unsurprisingly within minutes I found myself talking to the driver about the round ball game.

'Do you support Napoli,' I asked?

'No. I love Milan. I don't know why, but they have been my team from a young age. But as Napoli was close by, I often go to the stadium. In fact, I am taking my daughters to see their first Napoli game in a couple of weeks. I made sure I selected the more expensive seats away from the crazy fans and an early afternoon kick-off. I want to make sure my girls are safe, as it gets out of control at every single game there.'

'Do you follow Italian women's football too? I think it only turned professional recently?' I asked.

'No. I don't know much or even anything about women's football. I know from this year I can watch women's football games on television for the first time. But I haven't watched any. I am not interested. I associate men with scoring beautiful goals, not women!'

'That is an interesting perspective,' I said. 'I guess that's partly because you didn't grow up watching girls or women play football. It is a shame, as women can score beautiful goals too! What about tennis? Do you feel the same way about women's tennis?'

'I love tennis too. I am extremely proud and patriotic for Jannick Sinner—he is the first Italian to break into the top 10. We all love him here. It's rare for Italy to have a good tennis player!'

'And what about women's tennis?' I asked.

'Oh, I love Serena Williams. She is great. So powerful. An amazing woman.'

The driver went on to mention at least five female tennis stars that he liked and told me various reasons why he liked them. From power to grace to skill to strength to being the world number one.

'Do you know the names of any female footballers in the world?' I asked.

'Not one. I don't know any. I cannot tell you the name of one female footballer,' he said.

Conclusion: people need to be seen to be believed.

In case you missed it, just like women can hit wonderful shots on a tennis court, women can also score stunning, beautiful goals. Just saying.

And Then There Was Chess. Yes, Chess

Yes, chess. The sport that moved under the spotlight with the award-winning Netflix series, *The Queen's Gambit*. The one where we were all glued to our screens as the series took the world by storm. The one which showcased that women can be world class chess players, and that they can take on and beat the best men.

But suddenly, in September 2022, chess stole the headlines for other reasons. Ilya Smirin, chess commentator, was sacked for sexist comments made during a match.

The Israeli Grandmaster admitted on air that he had said chess is '*maybe not for women*'—and also seemingly praised a woman for playing like a man.

Belarusian-born Mr Smirin—who was once ranked one of the world's top 20 players—was making his debut as an English-language commentator in Astana, Kazakhstan.

He was initially speaking about one of the competitors, Chinese chess player Zhu Jiner. She is a woman Grandmaster, which is a separate, lower title to that of Grandmaster.

The commentators were discussing whether Zhu Jiner could become a Grandmaster when Mr Smirin said, *'She's a woman Grandmaster or what? ... Why she wants to be like men grandmaster in this case?'*

Mr Smirin went on to appear to admit that he had privately said, *'Chess is maybe not for women.'*

Fellow commentator Fiona Steil-Antoni said to him, *'You're saying, you know, "chess is maybe not for women,"'* and Mr Smirin replied, *'I didn't say it openly ... in private, private conversation.'*

And he also seemed to admit saying another female player—Grandmaster Aleksandra Goryachkin—had been '*playing like a man*'.

US women's chess champion Jennifer Shahade tweeted:

'Gross to see such sexism in the broadcast for a women's event ... Fiona did a great job in an uncomfortable convo she never should have been in.'

The International Chess Federation (FIDE) apologised 'unreservedly' and called the comments 'very embarrassing':

'Although we have great respect for Grandmaster Ilya Smirin as a chess player, the views he expressed on air are completely unacceptable, offensive, and do not represent any of the values that FIDE stands for,' it said in a statement, adding Mr Smirin *'will not continue as a FIDE commentator with immediate effect.'*

Checkmate.

Mr Smirin, however, told the BBC he was *'slightly puzzled'* as he *'did not say anything really bad, did not want to insult or hurt anyone.'* He said people had labelled him as *'racist, sexist and nationalist'* since.

'But what I said during the broadcasts was perhaps slightly impolite but nothing more,' he said. *'And the most of it clearly was*

a joke. If we will continue like that, the words "man" and "woman" risk to disappear rather soon. I want to stress that I did not want to hurt anyone, I love and respect chess and women. And I do not like hypocrisy.'[35]

It's not all doom and gloom though! There is a glimmer of light at the end of the tunnel.

In November 2022, Virgin Atlantic's CEO Shai Weiss claimed the company had seen job applications soar since they scrapped gendered uniforms.

He told *The Telegraph*: *'We saw a 100 percent uplift in applicants following the campaign, "See the world differently".'*

The firm launched its updated gender identity policy in September 2022, giving its crew, pilots and ground team the option to choose which of its iconic uniforms best represents them—regardless of their gender, gender identity or gender expression.

The announcement was part of an ongoing drive to champion the individuality of Virgin Atlantic's workforce, and the initiative was complemented by the rollout of optional pronoun badges for all its people and those travelling with the airline.

Launched as part of its 'Be Yourself' agenda, the airline has previously unveiled a series of industry-leading inclusivity initiatives for its people to ensure they can truly be themselves at work and feel comfortable in their roles. This latest addition follows a decision in 2019 to offer cabin crew the choice whether to wear make-up as well as the option to wear trousers and flat shoes. More recently, the airline lifted restrictions around allowing visible tattoos for crew members and its frontline workers.

This is backed by research conducted by 3Gem.

They found that enabling employees to express their true selves at work boosted happiness (65%), increased mental wellbeing (49%), created a more positive workplace culture (36%) and provided a better experience for customers (24%). Employees also reported feeling more accepted and comfortable when able to be their true selves at work (26%) and had an increased sense of loyalty to their employer (21%).

There are more reasons to get on board!

2019 data from the Limeade Institute found that when employees feel included at work, they are 28% more engaged and three times more likely to stay with the organisation.

Inclusivity can also have an impact on productivity. If employees are included at work and free to be themselves, then it is possible that they will feel happier. And, according to joint research from BT and Oxford University's Saïd Business School, workers are 13% more productive when happy.

Additionally, an inclusive working environment can also help with an organisation's recruitment and attraction strategy. For example, a Deloitte study recently found that 80% of more than 1,300 respondents said that inclusion efforts were a crucial factor for them when choosing a company.[36]

February 2022: Misogyny Prevails

In February 2022, Raith Rovers (a professional football club in Scotland) gave a contract to a convicted male rapist. This is toxic masculinity at its finest and a prime example of the misogyny that runs through the game. People running a football club made this decision—and to quote their reason published in their media release—*'first and foremost, this was a football-related decision.'*

Thankfully, the Board of the club reversed their decision some 24 hours later. But only because of public outcry, backlash and mounting external pressure from fans, players and the first minister of Scotland.[37]

Two days later, yet another story. This time in the Netherlands. Marc Overmars (former Arsenal and Barcelona football star) left his role at Ajax as director of football after it was revealed he sent a series of inappropriate messages to female colleagues over an extended period.[38]

It doesn't just happen in sport. Remember the spate of events in parliament in England in 2022?

'A top Tory was watching porn on his mobile phone in the House of Commons while sitting alongside a female minister.

'Three sources said that around a dozen female MPs at the meeting shared accounts of alleged sexism and harassment by their colleagues.

'One MP recounted how a female colleague in a knee-length leather skirt had been told by a male MP, "That's a nice outfit. What do you do for your day job?"

'Labour deputy leader Angela Rayner was accused of a Basic Instinct ploy to distract Boris Johnson at Prime Minister's Questions'[39]

This matters because when women see and hear these stories repeatedly, it will likely make them think twice about their career choices—after all, why would anyone choose to work in an environment where they are not respected?

What's the Solution?

It's complex. Given the prevalence of males dominating executive management positions, many companies are doing what they can in an effort to attract more women to apply for senior roles.

However, if we look beyond the surface and dig a little deeper, this strategy might not work. Why? Because in some instances, when women finally secure senior positions, they are still at risk of walking into a toxic, demeaning, 'male first, female second' culture.

Before fixing the quota tick box, organisations should perhaps consider addressing the root cause—their culture and values. If companies don't get this part right, they might well see a big initial spike representing an increase in females in senior roles, but it will likely be followed by a big downward line reflecting a big 'crash and burn—I'm not respected, I'm not valued, so I'm heading for the exit.'

And where would this leave organisations? Back to square one.

Mr Sepp Blatter

As someone so steeped in football, I could not ignore Sepp Blatter, who served as President of FIFA from 1998 to 2015.

His quote below is from 2004, but I don't think much has changed since then.

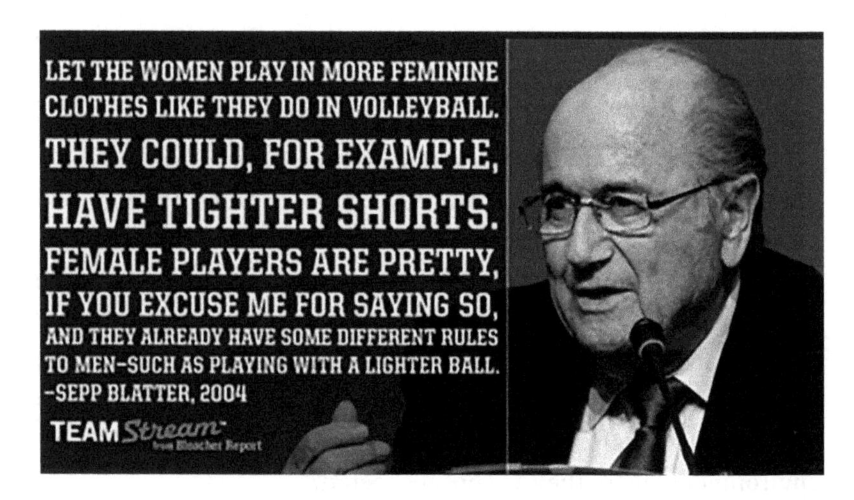

So, let that sink in: Blatter thought it was OK to tell the world that *'Female players are pretty,'* and *'They could, for example, have tighter shorts.'*

Backwards Not Forwards

If you think it is an exaggeration to suggest we are going backwards, not forwards, just look at what happened to the Norwegian beach handball team in 2021. They were fined for wearing athletic shorts instead of bikini bottoms in a bronze-medal match against Spain after officials deemed the shorts to be 'improper clothing'.

The Norwegians wore regulation-sized black bikini bottoms through most of the Beach Handball Euro 2021 tournament, but they pulled a last-minute switch ahead of their final match. The women walked out in tight-fitting blue athletic shorts, drawing cheers from the crowd and anger from the European Handball Federation (EHF), who fined all 10 players for a total penalty of €1,500.[40]

We only need to look at what happened in the United States of America in June 2022 with abortion rights for women to feel that for every baby step we take forward, we seem to take another one thousand back. The US Supreme Court overturned Roe v. Wade, the landmark piece of legislation that made access to an abortion a federal right in the United States. The decision dismantled 50 years of legal protection and paved the way for individual States to curtail or place an outright ban on abortion rights. Like many women around the world, I was outraged. It felt like 1942, not 2022. When will this stop? Please, show women the respect they deserve.

As Ruth Bader Ginsburg said, *'The decision whether or not to bear a child is central to a woman's life, to her wellbeing and dignity. It's a decision she must make for herself.'*[41]

And how about this one from Scotland in August 2022? This one came close to making the podium for me!

Judy Murray. I concur.[42]

At first, I was really happy to read the news about Scotland being the first country in the world to make sanitary products free. At last—common sense prevails. Why was I so happy? Because like many women, I have been caught on many occasions by a period coming unexpectedly (because hey, guess what, we don't always track our flow and even when we do, our cycles can do anything; the 'average' cycle length of 28 days can sometimes change to 21 days or 35 days or any other arbitrary number in between!).

So, on days like these, what did I do? I would reach for copious amounts of toilet roll and if I was wearing anything that was white or lightly coloured, I would usually try and plot my route to the nearest exit and get out of there as quickly as possible! On that note, I have never understood why in the female bathrooms of so many workplaces, there are zero sanitary products, even for sale.

I'm sure a lot of women will relate to this feeling; you're in the office, and wham bam, thank you, ma'am, 'hello period', out of nowhere. What do we do? We look around the office and try to find a route and a time (ideally when the office is empty or nearly empty) to another female's desk. Shall I, shan't I? Eventually, we decide to go ... now, let's get this mission done—we walk tentatively and discreetly towards another female's desk and whisper as quietly as possible—'Do you have "something"?' (Because we couldn't possibly say tampon in public, could we?) And then there's the whole handover. I'm sure from the outside it must look like an undercover drug smuggling manoeuvre! Why? Because we couldn't conceivably carry a visible tampon in our hands, so it's either handed to us in a little bag (in an effort to disguise the ghastly, disturbing content) or we shove it up our sleeve at rocket pace and then rapidly run away with our 'stolen' goods! It's such a shame that women feel so embarrassed about something which happens so regularly throughout their lives.

Anyway, back to Scotland. It was an amazing initiative. But then look what happened next. Guess who got the job to roll out this wonderful project. A man. Yes, a man got the job as 'period dignity officer'.

Now, don't get me wrong. I am in favour of the best person for the role getting any job, regardless of gender. But out of curiosity, do you think a man or a woman knows best when it comes to feeling blood seep through their knickers and run down their legs? I look forward to putting my application in for 'dick dignity officer'. I think I am the perfect match because I have all the credentials to get me the job.

October 4, 2022: A Dark Day for USA Women's Soccer

Abuse and misconduct 'had become systemic' in the United States' top-flight National Women's Soccer League (NWSL), an independent investigation found.

US Soccer-appointed Sally Yates and King & Spalding LLP conducted an independent inquiry, interviewing more than 200 NWSL players.

'Our investigation has revealed a league in which abuse and misconduct—verbal and emotional abuse and sexual misconduct—had become systemic, spanning multiple teams, coaches, and victims,' the Yates report said.

'Abuse in the NWSL is rooted in a deeper culture in women's soccer that normalises verbally abusive coaching and blurs boundaries between coaches and players.

'The players who have come forward to tell their stories have demonstrated great courage. It's now time that the institutions that failed them in the past listen to the players and enact the meaningful reform players deserve.'

US Soccer president Cindy Parlow Cone called the investigation's findings *'heartbreaking and deeply troubling'*.

The NWSL said it would immediately review the findings.

As well as examining claims against Riley, the report looked into allegations against two other coaches, Rory Dames and Northern Irishman, Christy Holly.[43]

Sadly, it feels like these stories are everywhere. And this one from Vivienne Miedema (Netherlands international) really nails it on the head:

← **Thread**

Miedema (via Helden #62): "The biggest problem in women's football is that people in higher-up positions within FIFA and UEFA, they are mainly elderly men. They say they want change, but don't really know how to start it. (cont.)

13:46 · 08.06.22 · Twitter Web App

51 Retweets **3** Quote Tweets **329** Likes

Vivianne Miedema. I concur.

Nikita Parris (England international) raises some valid points too:

'I think the most frustrating part is how people directly compare the men's and women's game because men and women, historically, physically, emotionally, mentally are different human beings. Men are built in a certain way that allows them to have power, more physical presence than women. When you try and compare the women's game

to the men's, and when people say the women's game is much slower—that's a real frustration, because people tend to directly compare and never see the beauty in the women's game.[44]

If you're only used to watching fast, physical men's football, women's football may look slower. But a football game (played by men or women) can be exciting for many reasons—tactics, passing and goals, to name a few. Think of a professional female 100-metre sprint—the women's finish times are slower than the men, but the women's race will often, rightly, be described as remarkable, amazing, fast, furious, energetic, strong and exciting. So, if it's okay to use those words to describe women's athletics, then why not use the same words for women's football?

You might also find some different reasons to like women's football—here's a couple of the reasons I like it: there is less diving and hardly any dramatic rolling around—you know how the men sometimes go to ground when, so often, the contact appears to be minimal, but yet they frequently follow their fall with an expertly crafted, Oscar-winning Hollywood-esque triple roll around whilst simultaneously grimacing, screaming, swearing and scowling—anyone would think they had been shot multiple times at point blank range. It happens in the women's game too—but thankfully it's nowhere near as dramatic or as often.

There is far less backchat and more respect for the referees in women's football too. Don't get me wrong, you still see players surrounding referees after contentious decisions, but in men's football this has become so ludicrous now that it regularly stops the game from flowing.

And lastly, women do also score beautiful, powerful, stunning goals that make you stop in your tracks and say—'wow'.

The importance of role models. If you can see it, you can be it. Well said, Judy Murray:

Tweet

This is why we need pictures of female role models in every educational establishment and sports club around the country. If you can see it.....

6:18 PM · May 6, 2022 · Twitter for iPhone

If you can see it …[45]

And let's compare this to what I saw (see picture below) when I went for a walk through a park in Nyon, Switzerland. It's a totem pole. Kids need to join the pieces in the correct order to make three different sports people. There was a tennis player, a footballer and a hockey player. And a little side note: all the characters were male.

Exhibit A: Totem pole in a playground

It's a small thing, and maybe I'm overthinking how important it is, but add this to the mix with stereotypical children's books where girls are often characterised as beautiful princesses who love to wear pretty pink dresses whilst boys are often described as strong, powerful, commanding heroes, and it seems reasonable to think we could maybe do a little bit better.

In October 2022, I went to Basel in Switzerland for the Swiss Indoors tennis tournament. I arrived early, so I went for a little stroll around the various merchandise outlets. I saw this:

Swiss indoor Basel tennis merchandise display

There is a male and female mannequin, but with my critical hat on, my immediate reaction was why is the female one only half a body and why is it so small? The male is a giant! And how lovely, the female is wearing pink and the male is wearing blue. Really? In 2022. Maybe I was being harsh and maybe there was nothing wrong with this, as after all, I was attending a male tennis tournament. And maybe there were simply no female trousers or shorts to promote. (More often than not, the female merchandise is an afterthought.) Or maybe the majority of spectators were male.

I don't know the reason, but if we are striving for equality, then this display shouts the opposite.

Did You Know? 'Girls Are More Emotional Than Men'

'And that's why when they concede a goal, they don't take it too well!'

Well, that's what Kenny Shiels, Northern Ireland women's manager, said in April 2022 in a post-match press conference after his team lost 5–0 to England:

'I'm sure you will have noticed if you go through the patterns—when a team concedes a goal, they concede a second one in a very, very short space of time, right through the whole spectrum of the women's game, because girls and women are more emotional than men. So, they take a goal going in not very well. When we went 1–0 down, we tried to slow it down to give them time to get that emotional imbalance out of their heads. That's an issue we have. Not just in Northern Ireland but all of the countries in the world. I shouldn't have told you that.'

Once again, an apology followed:

'Shiels has since apologised in a brief statement released by the Irish Football Association. "I wish to apologise for my comments made in the post-match press conference last night," he said. "I am sorry for the offence that they have caused. Last night was a special occasion for the women's game in Northern Ireland and I am proud to manage a group of players who are role models for so many girls, and boys, across the country. I am an advocate for the women's game and passionate about developing opportunities for women and girls to flourish."'[46]

The Icing on the Cake

The cherry on the top of the backward momentum came in November 2022 with this little gem of a story from *The Guardian* which highlighted the behaviour of some boys who attended Eton College.

'Eton College has apologised and "sanctioned" a number of pupils after allegations that a group of girls visiting from a nearby state school were subjected to misogynistic language, racial slurs and jeering.'[47]

The Cherry on Top, December 2022

The Prime Ministers of New Zealand and Finland met at a press conference in Auckland and dismissed a journalist's suggestion that they arranged a meeting because they are *'similar in age'.*

'Finland's Sanna Marin and New Zealand's Jacinda Ardern said they met because they are Prime Ministers, not because they are both young, female leaders.

Ms Ardern questioned if male leaders would have faced the same question.

'Ms Ardern interrupted the question to say that she wondered 'whether or not anyone ever asked Barack Obama and John Key if they met because they were of similar age'.

'Former US President Barack Obama and former New Zealand Prime Minister John Key were born within days of each other in 1961.'[48]

So, there you go, sexism is everywhere. Sport. Media. Politics. Playgrounds.

A Second Cherry, December 2022

Jeremy Clarkson (ex-Top Gear presenter and journalist) wrote a column for the British newspaper *The Sun* about Meghan Markle, the Duchess of Sussex, which rightly (in my opinion) provoked outcry online, with social media users labelling it 'vile', 'horrific' and 'abusive'.

Clarkson wrote that '*he loathed Meghan "on a cellular level". He said he was "dreaming of the day when she is made to parade naked through the streets of every town in Britain while the crowds chant, 'Shame!' and throw lumps of excrement at her."*

His own daughter, Emma Clarkson, went against her father's words with this statement on her social media:

'I want to make it very clear that I stand against everything my dad said about Meghan Markle and I remain standing in support of those who are targeted with online hatred.'

'Meanwhile, the British social activist and chief executive of the Five Foundation, Nimco Ali, wrote: "A young Black woman opens up about her struggle with suicidal thoughts as a result of the abuse she got from the media, and this is how some men in the media react. This is absolutely horrific."'[49]

When will this nonsense stop? These words are hurtful. They are misogynistic and vile. They leave real scars. And it's absolutely not okay to talk about women like this.

After endless backlash on social media, the man himself came out with a statement saying he had made a clumsy reference and he would try to be more careful in future. He wrote this on his Twitter account:

'Oh dear. I've rather put my foot in it. In a column I wrote about Meghan, I made a clumsy reference to a scene in Game of Thrones and this has gone down badly with a great many people. I'm horrified to have caused so much hurt and I shall be more careful in future.'[50]

I've always wondered why it is so hard for some people to say sorry when they've clearly f*&ked up?! Why do they never want to admit wrongdoing and instead, they choose to dig themselves deeper? I really don't get it. I mean, he wrote it, he reviewed it, he sent it to the editor, he most likely signed it off. He knew what he was writing.

It seems a member of parliament in Southampton agreed with me. She wrote a letter to the Sun saying:

'Enough is Enough. We cannot allow this type of behaviour to go unchecked any longer. We now demand action is taken against Mr Clarkson and an unreserved apology is issued to Ms Markle immediately. We further demand definitive action is taken so no article like this is ever published again.'[51]

The letter was countersigned by a further 60 MPs.

I sat behind Clarkson at the UEFA Champions League final in Porto in 2021 between Chelsea and Manchester City. Sadly, at the time, I was a little bit excited about spotting a celebrity. But after reading his abhorrent words, if I was to ever see this man again, I don't think I would be able to keep my mouth shut.

A Third Cherry!

In March 2023, our lovely friends at FIFA announced supermodel Adriana Lima as an official FIFA fan ambassador ahead of the 2023 Women's World Cup. FIFA president, Gianni Infantino said Lima, a former Victoria's Secret model, *'lives and breathes'* football and would be an *'excellent link'* between the sporting body and fans worldwide. Lima describes herself as a football fan but appears to have had no official involvement in the sport before now.[52]

So, here we are, yet again. Another completely tone-deaf decision by the powers that be. Cue backlash. Cue uproar. Déjà f ***ing vu.

Bonita Mersiades, a former head of corporate affairs at Football Australia who worked on Australia's 2018-2022 men's World Cup bid, said that the decision highlighted FIFA's values.

'FIFA's engagement of Ms Lima as their global fan ambassador demonstrates just how out of touch FIFA is with football's fanbase and just how much FIFA hasn't changed,' she wrote in a Tweet.

When I saw the news story, I thought, *wow, seriously?!* I mean, why not use a true football fan who isn't a supermodel. Perhaps someone that lives, breathes and loves football, because after all, last time I checked, football is the most loved sport on the planet with more fans than any other sport, and they are spread all over the world. Or, failing that, why not use one of the best world-class female players who ooze skill, class, strength and passion for the round ball game?! I guess the latter ideas would be logical. We know that logic and governing bodies don't often go hand in hand.

Sexism personified with one FIFA announcement, only months out from what will be the biggest Women's World Cup ever, with 32 teams taking part for the first time and interest at an all-time high. Ho hum. Perhaps we might get to hear Gianni say, *'Today, I feel like a supermodel!'*

Chapter 6

2022 UEFA Champions League Final, Paris

The 2022 Champions League final was held on 28 May between football giants Liverpool and Real Madrid. It was the biggest day in European football history. It promised to be an all-singing, all-dancing showpiece spectacular. But the promise was short-lived. The following day, frightening headlines took centre stage. There was poor planning, disorganisation, brutal policing and unruly fan behaviour reminiscent of Hillsborough, with some calling it a near disaster.

I was lucky, or unlucky (depending on which way you look at it), to be at this match. I had been to the Stade de France once before in 2016 for the Euro final between France and Portugal and the knowledge I gained from that trip somewhat prepared me for what to expect; I recalled that in 2016 the entry to the stadium was extremely chaotic, muddled and crazy.

I also remembered the area around the stadium was shabby, shady and dodgy, and I recollected that the walk into the stadium was disconcerting, with some memories of there often being no visible path or pavement for pedestrians. I had a vivid memory of when we had no choice but to climb up onto and over a rocky, uneven mound before we could cross a huge, dangerous highway. I remember thinking it felt incredibly unsafe with hundreds of fans walking on the side of main roads whilst cars sped in both directions. I said to my mum who was with me, 'It looks like they've built this stadium without a thought in the world for pedestrians. I mean, how did they think people would enter? Are we meant to fly in and land parachutes on the field?!'

Eventually, after weaving our way through the bedlam, we were channelled, shoved and pushed into some incredibly slow-moving queues, and from there, it took what felt like an eternity to finally arrive at our seats.

Understandably, with this experience under my belt from 2016, my thoughts in 2022 were that we must get there early.

On Champions League final matchday, in the centre of Paris we met some delightful, charming, outgoing, fun-loving Liverpool fans who were, understandably, extremely excited and enthusiastic for the big match. I recall one fan telling me it was their first time attending a Champions League match, and they still couldn't believe they were there—'Was this really real?' he said to me. 'We are so lucky to have tickets!'

They had travelled through the night on a ferry to get to Paris as they couldn't get a flight. They joked that they wouldn't be able to eat for a week as they had paid an outlandish sum of money for their travel, tickets and accommodation, but they didn't care one single bit.

We started to chat about logistics—what time should we aim to arrive at the stadium and what was the best way to get there? I mentioned I had been before in 2016 and it was beyond chaotic, so my advice was definitely to get there early! That's when they made us aware that a train strike had just been announced and it would likely take even longer than we had originally thought. Surely not even the French could go on strike on Champions League final day?

A quick search of our route on Google Maps and bam, there it was, in black and white—strike, strike, strike—instantaneously, a sea of bright-red alerts popped up: *'disruption likely'*. Not on one, but on *every* single possible route to the stadium. I was in disbelief.

With this news, we set off even earlier than planned and walked to Gare de Lyon (one of the main train stations in Paris). Despite the strike, there was still (according to Google Maps), supposedly one direct train running from there to the stadium. On arrival at the train station—think busy, think chaos, think confusion, think bafflement, think this definitely doesn't bode well!

There were countless television screens with little to no relevant information about the match, no visible signage anywhere and zero staff around to assist the thousands upon thousands of lost football fans. Some great planning right there. I mean, after all, it's only the biggest match in European football and we are at the main train station in Paris. Signage, anyone? Staff, anyone? Information, anyone?

After walking the length and breadth of the station whilst simultaneously battling my way through the boisterous crowds, I finally found a staff member—'Excuse me, which platform is it for the Stade de France, please?' I was met with a big, stunned, completely dumbfounded, blank look. Nothing. Anyone would think I had asked something about rocket science. 'The Champions League final? The football match?' Still, non-responsive.

'Merci, madame! Ne vous inquietez pas! Bonne journée!'

Sooner or later, through all the confusion, one way or another, we navigated our way to the correct train. We were on our way! We still had two and half hours before kick-off. Plenty of time to get there and get in.

On arrival, we walked towards the stadium. It was relatively calm until we reached the infamous tunnel where stewards were performing the first ticket check. With my event hat on, I immediately felt something wasn't right. 'I don't like this—it's far too narrow—it's a bottleneck already and it's two hours before kick-off. I would hate to see this in an hour.'

With hindsight, we were exceptionally lucky as we got through without much trouble, but had we arrived any later, we would have likely been among the many fans totally stuck in this ridiculously slender space.

We were sitting in the Real Madrid end (another blessing in disguise) and entered the stadium relatively easily (there were only a couple of tense moments in the queue where the entry gates were temporarily blocked). This is when the rumours about fake tickets started to rumble and I had seen one or two fans attempt to jump fences, but as yet, nothing too crazy. Once we were in our seats, the atmosphere started to build, but as we approached kick-off time, something quickly felt amiss; there were so many empty seats at the opposite end of the stadium. The Liverpool end.

I was glancing at my phone. Within seconds, I started to be fearful for my own safety. Every time I looked down, there was another message from a concerned friend or family member:

'Sally, please be careful.'

'They are using tear gas.'

'Are you OK?'

'They are reporting muggings. Thousands of Liverpool fans are stuck outside.'

'Kick-off is delayed.'

'How are you getting home? Be safe.'

'Did you have any trouble getting in?'

'Stay safe. Text me when you are back at your hotel.'

It felt like the outside world knew more than we did. All we knew from the inside was that the Liverpool end looked strangely sparse. And then the announcement that kick-off was delayed was displayed on the giant screens. It was such a shocking announcement for many reasons—firstly, it wasn't true. And secondly, it reeked of Hillsborough all over again.

As I browsed social media, it became evident that things were more than chaotic. Videos of police using tear gas started to appear and images of petrified fans were plentiful.

Instead of enjoying the build-up to the match, I started to plan my exit.

There I was, at the Champions League final and instead of enjoying the spectacle, I spent most of the first half thinking about how to get out of the stadium safely. I was scared.

Liverpool lost 1–0. I don't remember much about the match. I was too focused on planning our exit as more and more shocking stories started to appear about the near catastrophe.

We decided to watch the trophy lift and let the crowd disperse before making our exit. As we made our way down the stadium stairs and out onto the concourse, I held on to my small bag as if it contained the Crown Jewels. More stories of muggings, fights and knife attacks blew up on social media and I wanted to get out of there, safely, and as fast as possible.

Thankfully our walk to the train station was relatively calm and we waited only 10 minutes or so until boarding the train. I was relieved to get home safely and I remember sending the same text to all those who were worried.

'Back at the hotel safely. A night to forget. Goodnight.'

The next day I was angry. Why? Because it appeared nobody was learning a single thing. The writing was on the wall from the men's Euro less than one year ago. Yet here we were again. Déjà vu. Zero lessons learnt. Will there ever be any accountability? Will anyone get punished? Will anything ever change?

I kept reading stories that highlighted how lucky we were that once again, nobody died. Is this really how we judge success now? A football match is okay if nobody dies? It's absurd and extremely sad.

And then came the stories from *The Guardian* about cronyism. My heart sank, but I felt relieved to see that others were being brave and speaking the truth.

Thousands of lives had been put at risk and this was most likely partly linked to cronyism; people in senior security positions who were ultimately responsible for the safety of thousands of people had been hired despite their qualifications not stacking up. It was unethical. It was disgraceful. It was shameful. And worse still, they were blaming the fans and counterfeit tickets.

Yet, as the October 17, 2022, BBC *Panorama* documentary revealed, the fact that so many Liverpool fans had lived through the terrible tragedy of Hillsborough probably helped save another disaster. Why? Because they knew better than anyone the importance of staying calm. And poignantly, they knew what could happen if they didn't.

The Calm After the Storm

A few days later, UEFA apologised to fans. Better late than never. An independent investigation was launched. Oh, and by the way, you'll love this one; all staff who attended were also sent an 'apology' email. It said that if we would like to share our accounts of what we experienced and witnessed, we could send an email to a UEFA staff member who would then share it with the independent investigator.

I couldn't quite believe my eyes. If we would like to provide any information for the independent investigation, we should email it to a UEFA staff member. This didn't quite match the understanding I have of the word 'independent'.

Chapter 7

(F)unemployment

July 2022

I am officially unemployed. I had enough of the nonsense and broke down. Yes, the once independent, strong, resilient, football-loving, mad Sally, who supposedly had her 'dream' job, walked out of work. I finally said, 'Enough is enough.' Why? I decided I could no longer work for an organisation that repeatedly showed little respect for their staff and where the toxic culture perpetuated injustice after injustice. I kept trying to find a way, but it reached boiling point where my health simply became more important. I had talked to a brick wall for too long and I simply could not keep going back for more.

I took time out to really delve deep into my thoughts and I came to a stark conclusion: if your most passionate, dedicated, motivated, hard-working employees want out, something is likely wrong with the organisational culture. And despite my finest efforts to bring inspirational, innovative change, I had to be realistic: the chances of pigs flying were far, far higher than the likelihood of me becoming anything close to a beacon for change.

Eventually, the accumulation effect got the better of me when I was involved in running a large strategic communication workshop day for stakeholders across Europe. Early on in the day, I took a call from a senior Human Resources' staff member to discuss an opportunity that had been bubbling away in the background for a couple of months. The news was negative and voila, it was the bullseye. It tipped me over the edge; I felt frustrated, angry, upset and broken.

I somehow muddled my way through the day, but I do remember gasping for breath as I walked outside to try and gather my thoughts with tears in my eyes and my head in the clouds. I was lost. I was broken. I cried. When I arrived home, I wrote an email to the relevant stakeholders explaining I was sick, and that I would update everyone once I had seen a doctor.

When I described my feelings, emotions and the situation to the doctor, his response was 'Sally, don't worry at all, this is completely normal. Sadly, I see people with similar situations to you almost daily. Call it a burnout. Call it exhaustion. Call it stress. Call it what you want, but the most important thing for you now is to switch off and completely rest and recover.'

For two weeks, I did exactly that. I slept for what felt like forever. I relaxed for the first time in a long time. It felt like an enormous weight had been bewilderingly lifted off my shoulders. Breathe.

Don't get me wrong, I was hurting. I didn't want to stop working. I wanted to find a way to stay and continue the journey. I wanted to secure a permanent role. I had worked so hard to achieve my dream, but as many close friends and family told me, sometimes when your dreams come true, you realise it isn't quite what you dreamt of.

It was particularly hard, as if you haven't already realised, I love football. I even wrote a post about how much I missed football during the pandemic.

14 April 2020, LinkedIn Post

'Surviving without the beautiful game

Life without football is tough. However, I'm still finding ways to engage with the beautiful game ... read on to find out how!

Football has momentarily vanished, but life must go on.

Like many, football is a huge part of my life. I am an avid player, a massive fan, a passionate coach, an enthusiastic writer and I am also fortunate to currently be employed within marketing for the European governing body for the sport—UEFA.

Once upon a time, I had skills!

How are you still getting your football fix through the crisis?

I think like many others, at first, I was in denial. Surely all world football could not completely vanish. Or even if football stopped, there will be some other sport to watch on television. I couldn't get my head around the possibility that all world sport would come to a halt. However, the stark reality soon caught up with me. As the constant cancelled notifications appeared on my phone, it was clear—no longer could I watch my beloved Brighton and Hove Albion FC every weekend, no longer could I play football twice per week at lunchtime, no longer could I write about football, no longer would UEFA Euro 2020 take place this summer and so on. I felt angry, I felt frustrated. I felt sad. But eventually, after the denial and the annoyance, came acceptance.

To make the most out of this crazy, unprecedented situation, I am staying engaged with the beautiful game in many ways ...

Skills, take two.

PS I suggested this picture might be used for the front cover for this book, but the publisher rightly pointed out, I'm not a player, only a wannabe one!

I keep playing

I am lucky that I have a small front garden which has a wall! What's so important about a wall, I hear you say?! It means I can kick the ball against the wall ... right foot, left foot, different distances, different angles and so on. I have never appreciated a football and a wall so much! I am also lucky that I live one kilometre away from Prangins football field which is still open. It's a beautifully kept field on the lake with goals. With the stunning spring sunshine, I go there a couple of times per week and practise all by myself. It's good for the soul, good for the mind and good for the touch ... I guess!

Talking of touch, I have always been useless at keep ups, so I've set myself a goal to keep me motivated—by the end of all this corona madness I want to be able to do 50 keep ups. A little ambitious as I'm only at 20 now, but with so much time, I thought I may as well aim high!

I keep reading

I make sure I keep engaged with all the positive news stories from the football world as so many clubs are doing some remarkable things. Reading positive news and smiling right now is so important as our newsfeeds are often dominated by negative, scaremongering headlines which are not good for our mental health. Football clubs and federations around the world are showing us more than ever that we are a community. We are in this together. They are putting aside money. Forgetting about their often-selfish agendas. Whether it is raising money to purchase medical equipment, producing training videos about staying fit at home, donating tickets for health workers, freezing payments for fans, delivering food to the elderly and vulnerable, or using the sport's enormous reach to deliver vital health messages. The football community is clearly coming together as one.

I keep writing

Although I cannot write about live football, I am still writing. I am writing a daily diary about living through the madness. I am also co-ordinating a couple of e-newsletters for the UEFA women's football team and the UEFA ticketing team. I am writing some feature blogs for an online football magazine—normally I write about current football, but now I need to be creative and innovative about content ideas. Sport commentators are in the same position—Nick Heath has made me smile a lot over the last week—without sport to commentate on, he is commentating on daily life or the lack of! If you want a laugh, follow @NickHeathSport on Twitter.

I keep watching

Aren't we lucky that we have technology?! Thank you, YouTube! I've watched the highlights of Brighton in the FA Cup final. Don't believe me?! Google the 1983 FA Cup final! I've watched the highlights of Brighton securing promotion to the Premier League. I've looked back at photos of when I went to my first Brighton Premier League game—the game when Brighton beat Manchester United 1–0 to secure their Premier League status. Yes, underdogs really do beat the giants sometimes!

And I think I've rewatched every camera angle of the recent spectacular bicycle kick scored by Brighton's Alireza Jahanbaksh at least 10 times! I was lucky enough to be in the stadium to see the goal live and it sent shivers down my spine—I've never seen a goal that good in real time. Reliving it via YouTube doesn't give me goosebumps, but it makes me smile and it reminds me of why so many of us love the beautiful game.

There are few topics in the world that are universal—but I think football and food are two right now that are helping keep so many of us sane!

My Instagram feed is littered with so many happy recent football memories. Watching England v Czech Republic on my 39th birthday in March 2019 at Wembley was wonderful and a stark contrast to my recent 40th 'football free' birthday just last week! Taking my best friend's daughter to her first-ever game at the Etihad stadium in Manchester and seeing her face light up with joy as we entered—all of these memories are almost fairy-tale like and I'm grateful technology has made it so easy for all of us to remember and look back at happy times. Thank you, Instagram!

What other things are you doing to keep busy?

I'm cooking, I'm cleaning, I'm reading, I'm doing jigsaw puzzles! I'm running. I'm cycling. I'm studying French ... or trying to! I'm volunteering to help the elderly in Nyon. I'm checking in daily with my neighbours to see if they are OK. It's a question of whatever you can do, however you can help, whatever difference you can make, now's the time to do it.

I'm spending a lot of time on Google Hangouts, Zoom, Teams, Skype, WhatsApp and Houseparty talking to my friends and family around the world. Who knew there were so many options for a video call?! Most importantly, despite the abundance of free time, I am trying to stay positive.

What do you miss most about football?

I miss so many things. I think number one—I miss watching Brighton—before the corona madness we weren't doing too well—in fact Brighton were yet to win a game in 2020, but still safe in 15th place in the Premier League. I miss the emotional rollercoaster—the wins, the losses, the feeling of a 91st-minute winner. I miss watching Match of the Day. I miss watching the wonder goals. I miss watching the howlers. I miss debating the pundit's analysis. I miss the weekly banter with fellow Seagull fans (yes, there are a few of us!). I miss reading match reports. I miss reading transfer news.

I miss playing Premier League Fantasy and screaming at the television when the striker I had as my captain misses a sitter. I miss playing with my teammates. I miss the socialisation. I miss the feeling of scoring a goal. I miss the changing room banter. I miss feeling exhausted after a tough session.

I miss working at the UEFA office. I miss working on ticket promotion for UEFA Euro 2020. I moved to Switzerland from Australia in 2018 to work in what I considered my dream role at a dream organisation for a dream competition.

Fortunately, that dream has been a reality for the past 18 months. But now my dream has shifted; I dream that I can be part of the postponed tournament in 2021. And maybe we will have another one year to go party—it's my silver lining for now!

I miss the passionate football-themed, Monday morning coffee machine chats with my colleagues. I miss the fervent debates, the laughter, the sharing of delight from reliving a Brighton win to anyone who is half interested!

If you can't already tell, I cannot wait for the beautiful game to be back. One thing I know for certain; the return will be an occasion to cherish. It's hard to imagine it now, but I think when football comes back it will be a huge emotional release for so many of us. Right now, football and many things in life are paused, but when we get to press the play button on football, we will undoubtedly be jumping for joy for a long time.

And lastly, my injury time mantra …

One of the reasons we all love football is because of its unpredictability. Ironically and frustratingly right now, we cannot predict exactly when it will be back. But believe me, football will be back and when it is, football will unite us and bring us together in a more powerful, commanding way than ever before.

I am thinking of football as a bright, shining light at the end of the dark tunnel. I promise we will all meet again soon at the glowing light—and it will be the most magnificent, memorable, magical, beautiful round ball game-themed party we'll ever have been to. Stay strong, stay safe and stay home. I'll see you on the other side ... at the shining light.'

Job Searching

I have enough job-searching stories for another book. Here are some gems.

Ghosts. Invisible. Second-Class Citizens

Once over the anger, frustration, denial and whatever else my emotion bank threw at me, without much hesitation, I started to look for jobs—there were plenty out there. And with little effort at all, I had nine interviews in only two weeks. The nine interviews were across four major sport companies. Here's an outtake of the first interview in July 2022.

First question ...

Interviewer: Can you tell us a little bit about your professional background and your personal life?

I thought it was a bit strange to ask about my personal life so early on, so I weaved in some light personal information throughout my answer ...

'I was born in Edinburgh, I grew up in Brighton, I support Brighton and Hove Albion, I moved to Australia in 2007 as I received the only full academic scholarship to study a Master's in Sport Management.'

I then went on to focus on my career and my relevant experience in relation to the role.

In my mind, I'd answered the 'personal' side. But no, this wasn't enough. The next line of questions came faster than lightning.

Interviewer: So, are you at home right now or in an office? Do you live in Nyon alone or with your family?

Gosh. We had been on the call for less than five minutes. Reading between the lines, in my mind, what they were really asking ... do you have kids and/or are you about to have kids?

What has this got to do with whether I can do the job or not? Would men get asked the same questions? Of course not. And this was in 2022. When will this nonsense stop?

I had the same type of question in August 2018. I was humiliated and then almost four years later, it simply felt like déjà vu.

I received invites for second interviews from three organisations. They all involved a pre-interview written assessment that was substantial, often challenging and detailed... in other words, can you please do this piece of work, which would normally be a three-month project for us, in less than a week, or in some cases in less than 24 hours, and then please send us your responses as a PDF so we can '*assess your thinking*'? Or, more likely, so if we like it, we can use it, take the credit, not pay you and probably not even get back to you to let you know what we think of your work or whether you have progressed to the next stage.

All three second interviews were on over consecutive days. In each one, I was grilled by three or sometimes four white men. Each interview went well—'excellent answers, Sally. Wow, Sally, we didn't think of that. That was a fantastic presentation, Sally. That's outstanding, exceptional. You've covered everything. We don't have any questions', and so on.

You know where this is going. The following week, just like buses, the rejections all came at once.

The gold medal response (otherwise known as you're simply too good and we don't want to pay for your skills):

'You were brilliant, Sally, but we decided to go with a more junior person—we think you are overqualified for this position, and we are worried you might be bored quite quickly.'

Of course, this is nonsense. You knew my level of experience prior to interviewing me, so please don't waste my time.

The silver medal (otherwise known as I am a bit scared that you are actually better than me, you might show me up and steal my job):

'You have the same level of experience as me, so it wouldn't be fair for me to give you this role—we need someone a bit more junior,' (said the director of communication). 'Your salary expectations are rightly at the top end of our scale, but I think you should be aiming much higher.

There is no way I would even get an interview for a role at director level ... Or perhaps I should change my name to Sam Freedman on my CV and then maybe I might have a chance! And yes, I have the same level of experience as you, but you knew that at the time of my application. I should be aiming higher and asking for more money? Noted.

And the bronze medal (otherwise known as brutal, but at least, honest, feedback):

'You were brilliant and in our final two, but the only difference was that the successful candidate had relationships with politically important countries to us—that really was the only difference.'

I thanked them for their time, silently hung up and thought, *gosh, I am so sorry that I am not a second cousin, half-sister or a best friend of a friend's friend of a prince, princess or a politician. Noted. How silly of me. I will add that to my CV headline in bold italics for next time.*

Those who know me will tell you I am persistent. I get knocked down. I go again. Resilience runs through my veins. So, let's go again. Let's take a look at LinkedIn. Oh, exciting. I have a new message.

'Hi Sally,

Sorry for the delay getting back to you. Great to hear from you and your experience sounds perfect—my only concern being that you may be too senior for this role. My colleague is going to shortlist, so let's see where that gets to and either way, it would be great to chat.

Thanks.'

That excitement quickly changed to disappointment and frustration. It felt like a never-ending Catch-22 cycle where I was firmly and resolutely stuck between a rock and a hard place. If I aimed higher (as I constantly was told I should), I did not get interviews and you guessed it, if I aimed lower, I would get told, *'You are too experienced, too senior, overqualified, too expensive'* ... any of the above, take your pick!

So, can someone please tell me, how do I get a job?!

Even when I thought I was close, I learnt not to get my hopes up. Despite being told I had been shortlisted for one second interview where I was one of only four who had from over 850 applicants…

Off to my second interview I went; after all, it was only a six-hour round trip to get there, where I also had to complete an assessment and a presentation. It went really well. I was happy. I did my best. Nailed the assessment. No regrets. And on leaving, I thought I had a reasonable chance of securing employment. At the end of the interview, they told me I would hear by the end of the following week if I had been successful or not.

That date came and went. I chased the week after. I heard nothing. I waited another week and I chased again. I heard nothing. About four weeks after the promised date, I received an email at 10 p.m. one night; *'Hi Sally, are you available for a call tomorrow?'* Nothing else, nothing more.

Slightly confused, I replied and said I was on holiday, but I was available around 10 a.m. the next day for a call. I heard nothing. I chased again a few days later to ask for a call to understand the outcome. A virtual call was finally booked for the following week. Ten minutes before the anticipated call, I received a cancellation notification. No apology or explanation, just *'cancelled'*. And then another call was scheduled for the day after. #Shambles.

Finally, the call happened. I got clarity. The organisation was extremely sorry, but '*There has been a restructure and the role I applied for no longer existed in the new structure. We are terribly sorry, especially as we worked so hard to get this position signed off. We really are truly sorry—you were in our top two candidates. We have been spending all this time trying to find another way to get the budget, but it's impossible, so with that we have to say, cheerio and ciao.*'

On another occasion, after a second interview, I was told, *'We are going to act really quickly, you'll definitely hear from us before the end of this week.'* I was relieved as the end of the year was fast approaching. That end of week came and went. The following week, I chased. A vanilla, plainer than plain, soulless, *'We are still in the process of finalising our decision'* email landed in my inbox. Oh well, at least I had been acknowledged this time. And then at 5 p.m., on the last working day of the year, I received a text message to tell me I didn't get the job. Apparently, it was *'nothing to do with my personality or experience—quite the opposite, in fact.'*

What does that even mean? I thought. I probed a little bit further to understand the real reasons and was eventually told: *'You were too good for this role, too experienced, you were the best candidate we interviewed; in all honesty, the decision we took was slightly political.'* Honesty at last. But ouch!

Why do managers so often have such poor communication skills? How hard is it to talk to people? To deliver bad news? I guess mobile phones and online chat programs have made it even easier for people to hide behind screens. Delivering bad news via a keyboard offers an easy way out. Hit send and run. We've all done it. But please stop. Pick up the phone. Better still, meet the person face to face. Messages can be misconstrued. They hurt people. They can negatively impact mental health. Show some respect. Manage expectations. Keep candidates informed if timelines change. Deliver bad news. It really isn't rocket science.

October 2022—Salary Range Time

Another email regarding a job application arrived in my inbox:

'Before we progress your application, to be respectful of your skills and experience, please let us know your salary range.'

I hit reply and started with all the usual polite waffle ...

'Dear xx,

Many thanks for your email.

I wish to be paid fairly for my relevant skills and experience which I have gained over the last 20 years of employment. My last salary was xxxx plus bonus. And a quick Google search shows the average salary for a senior communication manager in Switzerland is xxxx. I trust this provides you with enough information.'

And then I typed, but promptly deleted:

'PS: How about, next time, **to be respectful** *to my time and energy and in the essence of transparency and fairness, you advertise the salary when you post the job advertisement?'*

I have never understood why so many job adverts do not include salary ranges. Be open. Be honest. Show integrity. It's common sense, fair and it will save you time. Otherwise, countless candidates will apply thinking that the salary is open for discussion. They will likely assume it's open for negotiation and they will, rightly, want to be paid fairly for their experience. Last time I checked, candidates are not psychic; they do not have special powers to magically find out what the salary is.

But no. Employers so often do not disclose this information, probably because they want to try and save a few thousand here and there. If they can get away with paying someone less than the allocated budget, then they will. It makes no sense, as so often, countless interviews happen over weeks, sometimes months and eventually the feared salary conversation comes up, quite repeatedly, as the final step. And guess what, hey presto, no agreement can be made, which simultaneously sends the recruiter back to square one and leaves the candidate frustrated yet again about a pointless, characterless, time-wasting, nonsense circus of a process. What a great return on investment that process was. Not.

I guess hiding salaries also makes it easier for the much-talked-about gender pay gap to continue. Even if it's not a conscious decision by the employer—if a woman gets the job, there is a strong chance she will be paid less than a male counterpart. Let the inequality pattern continue. Yawn, yawn.

Don't Believe Me?

Swissinfo reported in November 2022 that the gender pay gap in Switzerland is still among the biggest in Europe. In 2020, women earned on average 18.4% less than men for equivalent work, according to the figures.

In Switzerland, 75.4% of women aged 15 to 64 have a job. This is one of the highest rates in Europe after Iceland and the Netherlands.

The EU average is 63.4%. But the high Swiss rate is explained by the high percentage of women employed part-time in Switzerland (60.9% in 2021). The EU average is 28.8%.[53]

And if these statistics are not bad enough, a University of St Gallen report in September 2021 found that only 17% of top management posts are held by women and just 23% of middle management positions. Researchers analysed 320,000 employees in 90 Swiss companies.

'If we continue at the current rate, gender parity might become a reality two to three generations from now. Can we really afford to wait until 2078 and lose out on the tens of thousands of highly qualified women that get sieved out?' the report asked.

Not only are women winning fewer promotions at higher levels of management in Switzerland, but they also have a higher turnover rate within firms than their male counterparts.

This is despite recent legislation stipulating gender quotas for boards and executive positions at the biggest Swiss companies, and a requirement for big companies to publish gender pay reports.[54]

New Fad: Online Pre-Recorded Video Interviews

Welcome to the other latest fad which I love to hate—pre-recorded video interviews (apparently to make recruitment more efficient, fairer and less time-consuming for the employer), but for potential candidates, let me tell you—they feel terrible; like some ghastly, bland, all kind of weird and horrible 'event'. Why? Because, last time I checked, in everyday life, as humans, we are used to ***two-way*** conversations; they allow us to read body language which often provides us with cues to talk more, or talk less, to smile, to laugh or to pause. But in these ghastly, lifeless, artificial situations, we talk to a brick wall whilst staring at a massive version of ourselves speaking out loud. That's about as natural as the two artificial sweeteners my dad has in his tea.

For those of you who have never completed one—thank your lucky stars! In a recent one, I was first offered massive congratulations for making the 'cut' out of over 800 candidates. I was then informed that the interview should *only* take 20–25 minutes and therefore, please can I make sure I find a quiet space to complete it with an excellent internet connection (but please, whatever you do, don't use browser x,y or z as they won't work), please make sure I have plenty of natural light, and please can I complete this *small* step within 48 hours of receiving this email. If I don't, too bad, the video link will expire, and we will not consider your application.

In one of these absurd videos, I was met with four, over-enthusiastic 'heads of' who each threw me a 'quickfire' question as though they were auditioning for a recruitment reality show—and as they each finished their question, up popped a massive red 60-second countdown clock on the top right of the screen. Whilst I looked on, slightly puzzled, bewildered, and thinking to myself, *'what the actual f§"k is this nonsense?'*, I saw a massive reflection of myself as I was simultaneously instructed to start talking and reminded that I only had one minute to go—and, of course, I was expected to not get in the slightest bit distracted by the massive countdown clock, which now resembled a huge, red and white, giant flashy star, akin to an over-excited firework. If that wasn't enough, with 30 seconds to go, I was asked by a blue flashy firework, if I was 'done answering?' And if I went over the time slot, too bad. I was cut off mid-sentence. Hurry up, Sally. It's time for the next question.

I particularly like this sentence from a recent video interview invite:

'As much as we would have preferred to reach out to you personally at this stage, we are doing our best to make it a pleasant, fair and efficient process for all the candidates.'

Dear employers—please note, there is nothing pleasant about completing these hideous pre-recorded, unnatural, beyond preposterous, tiring and often irrelevant tasks.

The following image popped up in a LinkedIn post. It's so accurate. Good to know it's not just me.

LinkedIn delights take two.[55]

Ghosted

Even when I've met people face to face or had detailed and long phone conversations—or sometimes both—about a promised job and their reactions have often ended with something akin to *'Excellent, Sally, I think we can definitely make something work here—I'll talk to x, y and z and come back to you next week'*, next week comes and goes. Not a whisper. So, I politely get in touch based on our *'promising'* conversation from two weeks previously and then voila! You guessed it. Ghosted. How hard is it to be respectful? Even if it's a *'No'*, get back to people.

November 2022

Feeling like I was going nowhere fast, I signed up for a career plan webinar hosted by a Swiss recruitment expert. Within five minutes, the host presented some statistics and proudly exclaimed to the group: 'For every 100 CVs you send, you will be lucky to hear back from 20. And when I say hear back, that could be an automated rejection or an automated acknowledgement email.'

'Wow,' I said. 'That's shocking. How is that OK?'

"It is not OK, but it is life; to find a job, you need to play the hidden game really well, you need to tap into the unseen network as once a job is advertised, it is often too late, as it is likely that someone internally or externally already has it in the bag. It is just like the saying—it is not what you know, but who you know.'

Women and Underestimation

We've all heard anecdotes. When a man sees a job advert and he only meets maybe 50% of the selection criteria, he'll likely still apply and go for it as he will overestimate his ability to be able to somehow 'fudge' the 50% he doesn't know.

Conversely, women will often think, *'Oh, no, I can't possibly apply for that, I don't know how to do a few of the items on the list and I don't have the relevant experience for this or that.'* Even if women tick 90% of the 'must haves', they will likely focus on the 10% they don't have, which will more than justify their decision not to apply.

Recent studies have in fact shown that men of average intelligence think they are more intelligent than two-thirds of people, whilst women are more likely to measure their intelligence accurately.[56]

Perhaps if we want more intelligent decisions in life in general, then we should consider having more women on boards? Maybe?

Barriers to Success

I recently completed a survey about being a female working in sport. I was asked to what extent do the following statements prevent me from progressing in my career:

- *I feel disadvantaged because I don't get the new role/promotion opportunities men in the same roles get.*

- *I think I received fewer personal development opportunities than male colleagues.*
- *I feel like men are better connected in the sport industry and progress quicker and further in their careers.*
- *I believe I am paid less than men who do the same work.*
- *Male gate-keepers restrict my experience.*
- *There are not enough visible or vocal male allies in my workplace.*
- *As a woman, I don't have as many opportunities to play sport and as a result I don't feel that sport was an industry I could work in*
- *As a woman, I don't feel I can give 100% at times, when my body is going through natural cycles (menstruation, pregnancy, menopause).*

I clicked 'Strongly agree' on all of them!

I was also asked what one word describes what it is like to be a woman in the sport industry. My response was instant and easy.

Invisible.

Tall Poppy Syndrome

I first heard this term in Australia. And it rang a lot of bells.

What does it mean? In a workplace context it refers to this trend: instead of treating good staff as an asset, hiring managers see talented staff as a threat and then set out to make their lives hell. Looking back over my 20-year career, I can recall countless examples of this. It's horrible. It feels like bullying, and it crushes confidence.

Quietly Firing

Managers will often stop offering the employee opportunities to advance; stop inviting them to certain meetings; and stop providing them important work and feedback, often in an effort to 'belittle' them. These behaviours will often lead to unhappy, disengaged employees. Even worse, these staff are frequently the ones who started at the company with raw passion, energy, dedication, enthusiasm and plentiful expertise. They are also likely to be extremely conscientious, intelligent, engaged and loyal. Yet time and time again, companies do not seem to reward enthusiasm. Instead they achieve the complete opposite by doing everything they possibly can to push it away and suppress it, thus creating the perfect storm for a horrible 'us and them' toxic culture to permeate deeper and deeper.[57]

Quietly Quitting and the Great Resignation

It's perhaps no surprise that in 2022, we saw a new term enter the Oxford dictionary: 'quietly quitting'—it refers to a growing trend in the workplace.

During and post the pandemic, many employees began to feel like enough was enough; work-life balance came to the forefront of decisions. And with that, they decided to just do the bare minimum to get their jobs done—nothing more, nothing less. And if that didn't work, they quietly quit, for good.

I guess I am a proud member of the quietly quitting club. Anyone out there care to join me? It's quite a nice club! Promise.

The interviews that kept giving.

Another senior sport communication role. Another international, global sport federation.

At the end of the interview, 'Sally, do you have any questions for us?'.

'Yes. Can you please tell me the salary range for the role, as in the advert it only said competitive?'

'Oh, Sally. I am sorry, I do not have that information in front of me now. I do not know the envelope. But I would like to ask your expectations and your last salary?' asked the HR manager.

'Oh. I find that a bit strange', I said. 'It's a little puzzling that as the hiring manager for this position, you don't know what the budget is. But, anyway, I don't have any secrets. My last salary was xxxx and as I have nearly twenty years' experience, this is my ballpark as I wish to be paid fairly for my level of expertise'.

'OK. Thanks for that information. I can already tell you that's outside our range', replied the HR manager.

'Hang on a minute,' I thought. *'You just told me you didn't know the range? And now all of sudden, after I have given you a number, you miraculously found it or remembered it?! Thank you very much for*

lying to me. Great human resources' skills there.'

Just when you think it couldn't get any worse, it did. 'Sally, before you go, I have one more question'.

'Sure, what is it?' I asked.

'I can't find your date of birth on your CV?'

'That's because it is not on there and doesn't need to be on there! Why do you need to know my age?'

'Oh, it is for the Swiss blah blah, so I can calculate the Swiss blah blah,' said the HR manager.

'Wow. I am a little taken aback by your question as I have never been asked my age in any interview. But again, no secrets on my side. My date of birth is xxxxxx.'

'Thanks for your time. Goodbye'.

And that was me, officially broken. No resilience left. My tank had been running on low for a while with red warning lights continuously flashing. And unsurprisingly, after this not so lovely experience, it reached empty; akin to when your car jolts, shudders and then suddenly dies from no petrol. That was me. I was gradually fading and then quicker than lightning, I abruptly, completely froze.

Please. No more. I can't take this nonsense job search lark anymore.

Of course, I didn't want this job. From the moment I started the interview, I could tell the organisation was still in the 1950s as I was read verbatim HR policies from decades ago about the legal length of lunch breaks.

But my word. We are in 2023. For goodness' sake. I was speaking with a HR professional, who frighteningly by the way, had around 20 years' experience, but could not have a salary conversation and who asked me my age and demonstrated blatant age discrimination. I mean, get with the 21st century. Please.

Chapter 8

A Bittersweet Symphony: 2021 UEFA Women's Euro, England

England were crowned Women's Euro champions in July 2022. They went one step further than the men when they beat Germany in a nail-biting final 2–1 in front of a record-breaking crowd on home soil at Wembley Stadium. Cue—pure joy, pure celebration, pure pandemonium. England really were champions! No more years of hurt. And you know what? Seventeen million people in the UK tuned in to watch it. The media coverage went crazy—women's football was in the spotlight. Finally. Every headline. Every front page. Every major television channel!

For me, however, it was bittersweet. Why? Sweet because I was happy for England and the players. I was pleased for all the young girls and boys watching; they could finally see it to believe it—see what? See that women play football too, and you know what else, the England women are really, really good and you know what else? They are European champions. Drink. It. In.

But Why Bitter?

Because as a young girl, I was told assertively by my PE teacher at junior school that football was only for boys, and I could play netball or hockey. I covered what happened next in Chapter 1. (Quick recap, I rebelled—I went to play with the boys and as a result, I was punished and told to stand on the line.)

After the incredible victory by the England women's team, the players wrote an admirable letter to the UK Government requesting that every girl should be given the opportunity to play football at school (as currently at the time of writing, only 63% had the chance). When I read the letter, I felt mixed emotions; I felt frustrated, aggrieved and irritated:

- Why has it taken a trophy for people to want a slice of the cake?
- Why has it taken a trophy for people to start talking about women's football?
- What if England didn't win? Would the country be going crazy with coverage and giving the tournament so much airtime for many days after?

Probably not.

So yes, it was and is great; women's football was finally getting the attention it deserved, but it also hurt that it seemed to be only as a result of incredible success.

Put simply, women should not have to fight this hard for equality. Girls should have always been provided the opportunity to play football at school, not only in 2022 as a consequence of a European trophy. Don't get me wrong, it's wonderful what the women did—an absolutely amazing achievement, a landmark moment, and it will rightly go down in history for being the kick-start to monumental change that some of us have been crying out for for years.

As British politician Tracey Crouch powerfully said as the final whistle went, '*If you want a job done, ask a woman.*'[58]

Despite my bitter feelings, the triumph also evoked satisfaction, pleasure, happiness and empowerment. The women had achieved so much, especially considering the vast backdrop of inequality and insufficient funding that had surrounded women's football for so long.

And when Chloe Kelly celebrated her goal by taking off her shirt and racing around the pitch in her sports bra, it was a rare moment that said to the world, women are strong, commanding, powerful and athletic.

So, Women's Euro was superb. It was glorious. It was spectacular. It was breath-taking. But for me, personally, the overriding feeling was bitter-sweet—just like a juicy, grapefruit—sometimes they taste refreshing and delicious, yet simultaneously, they can miraculously make you experience a horrible wriggle and fidget frenzy as their overpowering sharpness sends shockwaves through your body!

And that's what I call a bitter-sweet symphony.

March 8, 2023

It was another International Women's Day and the theme for this one; 'Embrace Equity'. And on this day, the UK government finally did just that; they announced that hey, guess what? Girls will be able to play football in schools too.

Sky news reported:

'Schools in England will be told they must deliver at least two hours of Physical Education each week and that girls and boys should be able to play the same sports in lessons and extra-curricular clubs; this follows a campaign launched by England Women after their European Championship triumph last summer.

'Prime Minister Rishi Sunak added: "Last year the Lionesses' victory changed the game. Young girls know when they take to the pitch that football is for them and, thanks to the Lionesses, they too could be a part of the next generation to bring it home for their country."[59]

This is wonderful news. I am really happy for young girls living in England.

However, it still makes me incredibly angry that it has taken a European trophy to instigate change. Imagine if boys had to wait for the England men's team to win a trophy to be able to play football at school. Sounds ridiculous, right? And if the Lionesses hadn't won the trophy, would girls be waiting another 50 years? We'll never know, but you wouldn't count against it.

Chapter 9

The People's Game

September 27, 2022

Gary Neville needs little introduction; he's a world class football player, an England international, a manager, a pundit, a businessman and sometimes a vocal speaker about the United Kingdom's political landscape.

Gary was interviewed on the breakfast BBC news in late September 2022, where they covered a number of topical issues. Of particular interest, on the current state of football, Gary said:

'From the outside it looks all rosy and shiny, but in reality, we lack independence, fairness, a little bit like society. Football is a mirror of society. There should be a fairer distribution model, there should be full investment into the women's game, we should use football to address societal issues like racism and LGBTQ. All of these things can be done, but football has shown over the last 30 years that it can't come to those conclusions itself. It's no longer good enough to stay silent. We have stayed silent for too long on so many issues.'

It's Not Only Football

As Gary Neville said, football reflects society. Sexism is everywhere.

On the same day as Neville's football comments, Apple Chief Executive, Tim Cook, said there are still *'not enough women at the table'* at the world's tech firms—including his own.

Cook said technology *'will not achieve nearly what it could achieve'* without a more diverse workforce. ' *He said there were "no good excuses" for the lack of women in the sector.* Football world, are you listening?

'He said while companies including his own had made progress on diversity, there were 'no good excuses' for the tech sector not to employ more women. Football world, would you like to take note? Maybe this man knows a thing or two?

'Apple had 35% female staff across its global staff in 2021, according to its own diversity figures.

'One challenge facing the sector is the lack of girls choosing to pursue science, tech, engineering and maths subjects at school.

'Businesses can't cop out and say "there's not enough women taking computer science—therefore I can't hire enough",' said Mr Cook.

'We have to fundamentally change the number of people that are taking computer science and programming.'[60]

Sounds familiar. When I challenged some of my employers about the lack of female staff, I was often met with, 'Well, Sally, 95% of our applicants are men, so it's no wonder we mainly hire men.' With this attitude, nothing will ever change.

We need to find ways to firstly encourage more women to apply, and then when we get good female talent in organisations, we need to focus on finding ways to retain them. What does that look like? They need to feel valued. They need to have other female role models to aspire to. They need to be paid the same as their male counterparts who do the same roles. They need to be afforded the same opportunities as their male counterparts for promotions/

Ian Wright (Arsenal and England legend) summed it up perfectly, live on BBC.

'If girls cannot play football in their PE lessons at schools after this victory, then what are we doing? We've got to make sure they get to play and have the opportunities. This is as proud as I have ever felt of any England side.'[61]

Prize Money

This topic has dominated sporting headlines in recent years. Should women and men receive the same prize money? In tennis, they answered with yes. Absolutely. In golf too. In football, we are nowhere close.

Positively, women's football prize money has substantially risen in the last few years. For the Women's World Cup in Australia and New Zealand in 2023, there is speculation that the prize pot could rise to USD 100 million, up from $85 million in 2019.

Let's compare this to the recent men's World Cup in Qatar where FIFA set aside a whopping USD 440 million for prize payouts for the 2022 tournament, with $42 million going to Argentina, the winning team. The rest of the prize purse saw $30 million go to the runner-up (France), while the third-placed team (Croatia) took home $27 million. Coming in fourth earned the Moroccan team $25 million. Teams finishing 17th through 32nd received $9 million apiece, while those who made it to the round of 16 were guaranteed $13 million.[62]

In 2019, the United States women's winning team took home just $4 million—from a $30 million prize pool. The disparity led to US Soccer's decision to split prize money equally between the men's and women's teams through 2028.[63]

Yet, FIFA statutes stipulate non-discrimination on the grounds of gender.

Often, when I discuss this topic with male friends, they instantly come with the 'Yeah, but men's football is worth so much more, Sally, just look at the television rights, the sponsorship rights, the ticket sales – men's football brings more money in'. And I tell them, 'Yes, you're right. That's true'. But let's not forget, one of the likely reasons men's football is 'worth' so much more is because men have been afforded far more opportunities than women from the outset.

It's about time we make equal opportunities mean exactly that: provide men and women the same chances to play football, to watch football, to coach football, to work in football, and so on. But as this hasn't happened for so long, the gap is enormous, and women are going to be playing catch-up for a very long time.

So, what should we focus on now? We need to find and implement strategies to ensure the gap gets smaller and if that means paying women more in an attempt to bring some parity (not necessarily equality), then do it. This project is very much a marathon, not a sprint.

Marketing Mantra

I have a lot of male friends who love football and I often ask them their thoughts about women's football. 'Do they follow women's football? Do they know any players' names? Would they like to see more posts about women's football on social media?' And so often, the answers I receive are 'No, no and no'. I always ask, 'But why?' And the consistent reply: 'Because I am not the slightest bit interested in women's football. I've caught glimpses and it's slow and boring.'

But my next questions are: 'How can you become interested if you don't ever see, hear or read about it? Are you saying that nothing would change your mind and/or you have no desire to watch or care about women's football? Is it maybe because you are at saturation point with men's football? Right now, how much space is there in your free time to care about women's football too?'

These questions are met with a bit more positivity ...'Maybe Sally, you might have a point, but for now, I'm watching men's football and that's enough.'

How Do We Increase the Visibility of Women's Football?

- More female-focused social media posts?
- More female-led interviews?
- More females reporting, presenting and commentating on football?
- Increase the broadcast rights for women's games?
- Host more women's games in big stadiums?

None of these ideas are rocket science and some are already happening, but there is still a long way to go, and the extent of women's football coverage varies hugely depending on the country.

But Maybe It Isn't That Remarkable After All

I was chatting to a male friend whilst walking by the lake in Nyon in October 2022 and the conversation quickly moved to football and the upcoming men's World Cup in Qatar. As my friend was a local, I asked his advice for the best places to watch games. He didn't know. He said football really wasn't that big in Switzerland and he had read that the planned fan zone in the centre of Geneva had been cancelled; the company organising it had received too many threats about supporting a tournament in a country that had so much wrong when it came to human rights.

Out of curiosity, I asked him if he knew where the Women's World Cup would be in 2023 (Switzerland is in it). He didn't know. I asked if he knew Switzerland is going to be in it (the final draw had just taken place). He didn't know. I asked him if he could name any female footballer in the world. He looked at me blankly and said, 'No, not one, but I can give you five female tennis players.' I asked if he would like to know who Switzerland would be playing? He wasn't interested, but I told him anyway! (Philippines, New Zealand and Norway in the group stage).

Perhaps 'forced', token female-focused social media posts are not ideal, but it's often a directive from above that we need to push women's football to strive for equality, so if that means three times female-focused posts per week, it's a tick box that is relatively easy to achieve.

In England, we are seeing more and more females involved in football media and more coverage of women's football than I can ever remember. Women's football attendances are also growing and growing. When England won the UEFA Women's Euro, the story dominated the television news headlines across multiple channels, and the players were rightly splashed on the front pages of newspapers. This has to help. Even if you weren't particularly interested, it's likely that at some point on the day after the final you will have read, listened or watched something about the victory.

Admittedly, marketing is only one part of the strategy—setting up more options for young girls to play is arguably even more critical, but I also believe that the millions of football-loving men and women out there would maybe become slightly more interested in women's football if they only knew a little bit more about it and were exposed to it more regularly. As the late Queen Elizabeth II once famously said, *'I have to be seen to be believed.'* She wasn't wrong.

Sponsorship

October 17, 2022

Ballon d'Or—a picture paints a thousand words. So does a caption.

BBC SPORT

Ballon d'Or photocall at Theatre Du Chatelet In Paris

PARIS, FRANCE - OCTOBER 17: Vivianne Miedema (L) and a guest attend the Ballon d'Or photocall at Theatre Du Chatelet In Paris on October 17, 2022 in Paris, France. (Photo by Marc Piasecki/WireImage)

Vivianne is happy she got to take her 'guest'

Vivianne Miedema is pictured with England international and UEFA Euro 2021 winner, Beth Mead. Yet, poignantly, the caption reads 'Vivianne Miedema and a *guest'.* I'm not even going to go there. Or maybe I will. For those who don't know, Beth Mead also came second in the Ballon d'Or awards on that evening for the best football player in the world.

Hats off to the girls for making it comical and seeing the funny side! Can you imagine the same for a picture of Ronaldo and Messi captioned with 'Messi and guest'?! No, nor can I!

Admittedly, whoever wrote the caption probably didn't know who Beth Mead is. Does that make it okay? No. Absolutely not. All it shows is that despite there being a huge increase in the visibility of female footballers, there is still a long way to go.

Positive Discrimination

When I talk to my male friends about these issues, positive discrimination comes up time and time again.

'But Sally, I know loads of men who can't get jobs now because women are getting them just to tick boxes, it's really not fair.'

My reply is usually along the lines of 'welcome to our world'.

On the flipside, I do believe the best person should get the job no matter their gender, race, age, religious beliefs and so on. There are very few women who want a job only to fill a quota. But they do want to be recognised for their skills and afforded the same opportunities as men.

As women, we have to fight even harder for that job, that promotion, and for a seat at the table. At football matches, we need to prove we know every last inch of the offside rule before men will give us the time of day. It's wearing.

Parity in 140 years. Ouch. [64]

Did You Know?

The world's fastest growing 'language' is emojis. Yes, those lovely little characters that you most likely use daily when you send messages to your friends and family. And guess what? Until 2016, they were predominantly male-based emojis. And guess what else? Females are the biggest users of emojis.[65]

And when it comes to news media—guess what? In 2015, the Global Media Monitoring Project reported that women make up only 24% of the persons heard, read about or seen in newspaper television and radio news, exactly the same percentage as they did in 2010.[66]

The same pattern is everywhere: banknotes, textbooks, statues, science. I could go on as the list is endless.

When it comes to sporting statues in the UK, a *Sky Sports* news investigation in 2022 found only three female statues, representing less than 2% of all UK sport statues: the three are of former England footballer Lily Parr, two-time Wimbledon champion Dorothy Round and Olympic pentathlon winner Lady Mary Peters.[67]

Remember the interview with Andy Murray where a reporter told him he was the first person to win two Olympic Gold medals? He replied that Venus and Serena Williams had won about four each. Or how about in the USA, where so often people casually declare that the USA has never won the World Cup. But they have. The women have won an incredible four times. Not one, or two or three, but *four* times.

Do you believe me now that women are, at times, invisible? In fact, sometimes, it feels that we are working our way back to 1921. What do I mean? This.

'Complaints having been made as to football being played by women, the FA Council feel impelled to express their strong opinion that the game of football is quite unsuitable for females and ought not to be encouraged ... the council requests that clubs belonging to the Football Association refuse the use of their grounds for such matches.'

FA Council, 1921[68]

I know so many women who have told me they would have loved to have played more football, but there just were not any teams for them to join. So many women have missed out. For an incredible 50 years, women's football was suppressed in England. And now we are playing catch-up in so many aspects of the game. Learning, skills, opportunities, visibility, and so the list could go on and on and on.

Or how about the friend who recently told me her young boys had become obsessed with football during the men's Euro and begged her to subscribe to the *Match of the Day* magazine. Eventually she caved and to keep the kids interested and engaged, she bought them a subscription. Whilst on the phone to me, my friend flicked through the magazine, and she said she couldn't believe how few women were featured. Fifty pages for the men and two for the women. Sounds about right. Oh, and there were some League tables too. The English Premier League table was front and centre, then the Championship, League One and League Two.

Then there was the Women's Super League. The smallest of them all—a tiny little image concealed in the corner of the page. How lovely. And sorry to all those Scottish readers too; the Scottish Women's Premier League table was a similarly small size. I was born in Scotland. As a Scottish woman, I think I might cry.

My last anecdote comes from a webinar that I joined in May 2022 along with a number of other female professionals working in sport. We had five-minute breakout rooms to discuss sexism. One woman in my virtual room told a story of how her young girl will likely never play football again. Why? Because she had a terrible experience at a recent Premier League football camp held during the holidays. It went something like this: her five-year-old daughter was the only girl and she asked one of the coaches to take her to the toilet. There were no female coaches. The male coaches would not take her, or rather could not take her. And because there was no suitable woman present, the little girl wet herself and consequently, she never wants to play football again. Ouch.

Chapter 10

2022 FIFA World Cup, Qatar

November 19, 2022

It's two days before the biggest tournament in the world kicks off. I'm usually like a kid in a candy store at this moment in time. I'm nervous. I'm excited. I cannot wait for it to start. But this one felt different. I had mixed feelings. I was looking forward to watching the games but at the same time, like many others, I felt sad about the issues that were dominating the headlines and, in some way, overshadowing the much-anticipated spectacle.

On this day, FIFA president, Mr Gianni Infantino, hosted a press conference. Within minutes of opening, Infantino told the world he felt Arab, he felt gay, he felt disabled, he felt like a migrant worker, and he also said he knew what it was like to be discriminated against because he was bullied at school for having red hair and freckles. Cue uproar, perplexity and bewilderment.[69]

And isn't it ironic, don't you think, that only a few days before, Infantino had written a letter to all federations and teams asking them to focus on the World Cup football rather than on human rights?

As I listened, I was confused. It was incredibly bizarre. How could he be so disrespectful?

My football communication work brain went into overdrive; *who on this planet wrote this speech?! Did he write it himself? Or did someone close to him advise him that these words would be good to speak aloud? And my last thought: is this man all right?* Maybe he had lost touch with reality as his address, at times, came across as a confused, muddled, weird mess.

One Love Armbands

On the second day of the tournament, I watched England play Iran, Senegal play Netherlands and Wales take on the United States of America. F(unemployment) has its benefits!

The day started with more talk about captains' armbands than football. Why? Seven European captains were set to wear 'One Love' armbands (representing a positive message supporting the LGBT+ population and inclusion). FIFA were told about this initiative three months before kick-off, and they said nothing. But on the eve of England's first match, in true FIFA style, they piped up and said if players wore them, they would get booked and possibly face further disciplinary action. FIFA 1–seven nations 0.

'In a statement on Monday, England's football governing body, the Football Association and its Welsh equivalent joined the Netherlands, Switzerland, Germany, Denmark, and Belgium to confirm that threats of sporting sanctions from FIFA left them no choice but to abandon the One Love campaign gesture.

"As national federations we can't let our players face sporting sanctions including bookings, so we have asked our captains not to wear the armbands in FIFA World Cup games."

'They added that they were prepared to face fines for breaching kit regulations but they could not afford to have players receive yellow cards or be forced to leave the field.

'The statement also said the teams are "very frustrated with FIFA, and believe this is unprecedented", before noting that they will show support "in other ways."'[70]

'Woman, Life, Freedom'

Iran players chose to remain silent during their national anthem in an apparent show of support to protestors back home. The demonstrations were sparked by the death of Amini, the 22-year-old woman who was in custody after being arrested by Iran's morality police. She was detained for not properly covering her hair with a headscarf, or hijab.

'"We have to accept that the conditions in our country are not right and our people are not happy," Iran captain Ehsan Hajisafi told reporters at a press conference. "We are here, but it does not mean that we should not be their voice or we should not respect them."'

'Some fans in Doha wore t-shirts and waved signs saying "Woman, Life, Freedom", which has become a mantra of the uprising.'[71]

Seems it is not only at the stadiums, but also at press conferences too; when I browsed Twitter, this was the first tweet on November 21 to pop up in my feed:

'It shouldn't still shock me but the lack of female reporters in these press conferences at the World Cup is mind blowing. I have definitely sat with full rows of men in the last three of them.'[72]

Invisible women exhibit no. 3249856093768457658941!

But Don't Forget, Football Is for Everyone. It Has the Power to Unite, Said FIFA

But according to the Jerusalem Post:

'Jewish organisations said that even though they were promised otherwise, Qatar won't allow any cooked kosher food to be sold or offered to visitors of the FIFA World Cup.

'Qatar broke another promise to allow Jewish prayer services in Doha during the games, claiming it couldn't secure this type of activity and then banned it completely.'[73]

For the thousands of religious Jews set to attend the World Cup, I would take a wild guess that this news made their attendance impossible.

But don't forget, everyone is welcome...

November 23, 2022

Germany faced Japan. Another thrilling game, but guess what? Yes, yet again, the headlines focused on other issues.

Captain Manuel Neuer decided to wear the 'One Love' armband, along with German interior minister, Nancy Fraser, who was sitting next to FIFA president, Gianni Infantino, in the VVIP stand.

Additionally, the entire German team posed for a pre-match photo with their hands over their mouths to symbolise that they had been silenced by FIFA.

German football team pre-match photo. Shh.[74]

A German Football Association (DFB) statement said, 'We wanted to use our captain's armband to take a stand for values that we hold in the Germany national team: diversity and mutual respect. Together with other nations, we wanted our voice to be heard. It wasn't about making a political statement—human rights are non-negotiable. That should be taken for granted, but it still isn't the case. That's why this message is so important to us. Denying us the armband is the same as denying us a voice. We stand by our position.'[75]

November 24, 2022

Portugal 3 Ghana 2

Cristiano Ronaldo scored Portugal's first from the spot. Cue the plentiful, never-ending headlines informing me that Ronaldo is now the first player to score in five World Cups. Here's a tasty selection pack for you below: (taken from a quick Google search on November 25, 2022).

CRISTIANO RONALDO IS THE FIRST PLAYER TO SCORE AT FIVE WORLD CUPS

Cristiano Ronaldo makes history as first player to score in five World Cups with Ghana goal

Ronaldo delights.

https://sportstar.thehindu.com › news › article66179508

Ronaldo becomes first player to score in five FIFA World Cup editions

Cristiano Ronaldo became the first-ever player to score at five World Cups during Portugal's Group H opener against Ghana at Stadium 974 in Doha, Qatar on Thursday.
17 hours ago

These headlines are, of course, incorrect. Ronaldo is the first *male* player to score in five World Cups.

Two women have been there and done that. Brazilian Marta Viera da Silva and Canadian Christine Sinclair were already members of that exclusive club.

I particularly loved this article which led with the headline:

Ronaldo headline winner.

WORLD CUP 2022

Cristiano Ronaldo becomes the first player to score in 5 separate World Cup finals

And in the same article, at the very bottom (symbolism right there), it said this:

'In the ***Women's World Cup, Marta Viera da Silva*** *(2003, 2007,*

2011, 2015, 2019), and **Christine Sinclair** *(2003, 2007, 2011, 2015, 2019) have both scored in five separate World Cups.'*[76]

So, there are two apparently almost 'invisible' players who have already achieved this feat.

Wouldn't it be simpler to type a four-letter word in the headline? The first ***'m a l e'*** player to score in five separate World Cup finals? It really isn't that hard or offensive, is it? Or if that option doesn't take your fancy, you could add a 'men's' in front of 'World Cup'. Either work. The choice is yours.

December 4, 2022

Olivier Giroud became France's leading all-time ***men's*** goal scorer. I think by now you know what's coming next.

Another one for the record books.[77]

For the record, Eugénie Le Sommer (86 goals in 175 caps) is STILL France's all-time leading goal scorer.

Olivier Giroud (52) passes Thierry Henry (51) as France's all time leading men's goal scorer.

4:50 PM · Dec 4, 2022

2,088 Retweets **203** Quote Tweets **11.3K** Likes

It's really not that hard to get it right. Just add the word 'men's' and voilà—no more complaining!

Magic. One word makes all the difference: 'men's'. [78]

Olivier Giroud scores his 52nd goal for France (in 117 caps) becoming the all time top scorer in France men football history, passing Thierry Henry! What a record to break! Record breaker, history maker! @ESPNFC @_OlivierGiroud_

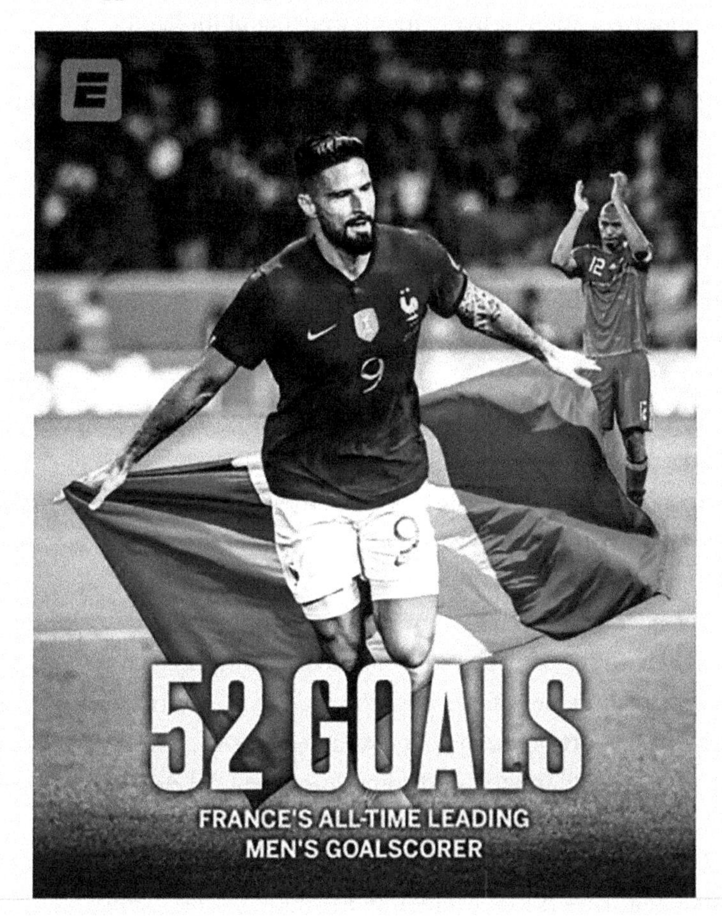

On the same day, ITV commentators said, *'We haven't heard the song "Sweet Caroline" for 15 months'*—this was true in men's football, but by not adding the word men's it casually discounted the women who won the women's Euro only six months earlier, when we heard

Sweet Caroline on repeat as the women were (in case you missed it) triumphant in beating Germany in the Euro final at Wembley.

This casual statement caused more uproar on social media. I don't think the commentator had any bad intention and most likely, he meant that we hadn't heard *Sweet Caroline* for a long time in men's football, which was correct and fair. Sometimes, I do think we need to calm down, and not make mountains out of molehills.

But it is still slightly frustrating, as this could easily be fixed by calling the World Cup "the men's World Cup", by calling Euro "men's Euro" and by calling the Champions League "the men's Champions League". If this was 'normal', then there would be no need to have a debate about sexism when referring to top goal scorers.

This is why I praise the Australian Professional Leagues (APL), who in September 2021 decided to rename their leagues "A-League Men", "A-League Women" and "A-League Youth".

Why? It means that the national women's competition will no longer be called the W-League. It was a move to strengthen gender equality in Australian football.

According to the A-League's CEO, the A-League's brand is *'aimed at a more equitable approach and tapping into the country's youngest and most diverse fan base'*.[79]

But back to the 2022 World Cup. It was a rollercoaster like no other. The highs, the lows and the surprises were synonymous with the beautiful game, and undeniably is one of the reasons why it is the biggest sport on the planet—we never know what might happen. The underdogs can win, and sometimes they do! And the joy which comes from that unpredictability is enormous.

This World Cup showed us that on match day two when Saudi Arabia beat Argentina. I remember thinking—*wow, finally we have a football-themed story to talk about. No more armband headlines. Thank you, Saudi Arabia!*

But this World Cup threw up a new giant, constant, uncomfortable and bumpy narrative onto our normally only football-fuelled rollercoaster ride; the never-ending painful human rights stories, sometimes rightly took centre stage.

Anyway, back to football. I don't like to think too much about the bumps.

The Last Dance, December 18, 2022. Argentina vs France. Messi vs Mbappé

What a final. It was the best World Cup final I have ever seen.

It was like watching a magical, incredible, wonderful and beautiful imaginary game of football, yet it was real. It was spectacular from start to finish: the flawless, perfect, immaculate number 10 for the last dance.

In case you were sleeping under a rock, Argentina won the World Cup for the third time in their history. In case you were not one of the billions who watched, it ended 3–3 after extra time, and after a game of tic-tac-toe between Messi and Mbappé. Cue penalties. Argentina won the shoot-out 4–2. Remarkable. Cue tears. Cue unbounded joy. Cue beeping horns (even in sleepy Switzerland!). Cue all-night-long celebrations.

Something you may have missed; Argentina's second goal was a sublime team goal, and it was assisted by a Brighton and Hove Albion player—yes, you read that correctly—little old Brighton now have a World Cup winner in their squad. Take a bow, Alec Mac Allister. Simply magnificent.

I mean, really, how do some people not like football?!

So that was it. Finito. The final curtain was pulled over Qatar. It was controversial. It was memorable. But my gosh, we were all reminded of why we love the beautiful game so much with an incredible, magnificent, wonderful, fairy-tale-like final that will forever live in the memory bank. And I'm quite sure we will ever see anything like that again. So, a huge merci to France. And an even bigger gracias to Argentina.

Don't cry for me, Argentina. Unless they are tears of joy. Thrilling. Amazing. Wonderful. Delightful. Splendid. Incredible. Destiny for Messi.

Despite all the controversy, the Qatar World Cup ended on an epic high. Fans were treated to an all-singing, all-dancing finale that showcased the beautiful game to be just that. It was gorgeous from start to finish. It was exciting, breath-taking, spectacular and unpredictable.

And, for me, it served as a poignant reminder that the game of football really is truly remarkable. It has the power to unite people, like nothing else. The live scenes from Argentina after the final whistle were magical. The streets were filled with so much noise, colour, passion and pride. There were tears of joy everywhere you looked. Unbounded happiness. Limitless love. On this day, it felt like football was the real winner: football 1–controversial news stories 0.

Over to you, USA, Mexico and Canada.

Chapter 11

Injury Time Mantra

Enough is enough. Viewing men as the default human is damaging. It's time for women to be seen and to be heard.

To all those who think sexism doesn't exist, I hope these stories have given you some insight into the reality, prevalence, importance and seriousness of the wide range of sexist issues.

What's the Solution?

I wish I had all the answers. Like many, I don't. I guess writing this book is my attempt at trying my best to solve this extremely complex jigsaw puzzle.

I do know that we need to speak up and we need to do more around educating key leaders and decision-makers so we can at least collectively try and decrease the occurrences of sexism.

February 2023

Speaking up is essential and it works. A recent example of misogyny comes from the Welsh Rugby Union, and it was uncovered in a BBC one-hour documentary.

'Women who for 30 years remained silent about the misogyny they say they faced while working in sport have shared their stories following allegations made against the Welsh Rugby Union.

'The allegations have prompted other women to speak out for the first time.

'Cath, who does not wish to give her surname, worked as a press officer for the WRU in the late '90s when she was in her 20s.

"I was absolutely astounded at the amount of sexism I saw there, it

was just all day, every day," she said.

"It was often from committee members and from the people right at the top."

'Jane Anderson was a national development officer with the Sports Council for Wales, now Sports Wales, and was based at Sophia Gardens in Cardiff between 1991 and 1993.

'She said on a training day shortly after she took up the role, she was made to feel very uncomfortable by a delegate from the WRU.

"The person in question leaned across the table to me and said 'how long does it take to get your knickers off?'

"I was so surprised I thought perhaps I'd misheard him and I said 'pardon?' and he repeated it again.

"So, I just collected all my bits and papers in front of me and moved to another table."'[80]

As more stories come to light, I hope more women will be encouraged to speak up, too. Sometimes, I feel dismayed when sexism scandals dominate the headlines day after day, as some of the stories are often confrontational and upsetting; would it be easier not to listen? To brush them under the carpet and deny all knowledge? Probably, yes.

However, these news stories play a vital part in changing the narrative, in education and in raising awareness. Put simply, with increased storytelling, particularly those stories that focus on liability and penalties for those in the wrong, people will likely feel more comfortable to call sexism out and challenge it. Think of it like a flow chart.

1. Women tell their stories, which encourages others to do the same.

↓

2. Media amplifies the stories, which raises awareness and education around the key issues.

↓

3. The media focus on stories linked to accountability and punishments for those in the wrong.

↓

4. More people become aware of various forms of sexism and possible consequences.

↓

5. More people feel happy to call sexism out.

↓

6. Less instances of sexism occur, as more people are educated around what it is and why it is wrong.

↓

7. Sexism decreases and women take a small step towards equality.

And maybe, slowly but surely, shocking news stories like the one above will be a rarity rather than the norm. However, women speaking up and increased news coverage are only parts of this very complex equation. Many other initiatives are required too.

A Roadmap to Gender Equality

I'm not a fan of quotas and hiring females just to tick a box, but we do need to implement fair strategies that are aimed at moving towards equity. For example, let's stop with the 'but only men applied' chestnut and let's instead, crack open the champagne—how? Let's try and fix the cause by implementing strategies that are designed and aimed at specifically attracting more female applications. Create more job websites that target women. Hold female-only networking events. Support and encourage women to apply for senior roles internally.

McKinsey Report—Women in the Workplace, 2022

This is the largest study on the state of women in corporate America. Between 2015 and 2022, over 810 companies and more than 400,000 people participated in the study which was aimed at giving companies insights and tools to advance gender diversity in the workplace.

What Did the 2022 Report Find?

For companies to be successful, they need to actively try to get more women into leadership roles and also focus on implementing strategies that aim to retain their current female leaders. The report also suggested leaders should be held accountable—these strategies should not be 'tick-box' key performance indicators discussed once a year in performance reviews, but instead should be regularly discussed, monitored and tracked. Additionally, companies should implement training for all staff around discrimination (not just sexism), with the intention of showing staff how they can call discrimination out and practise allyship.

Catering the workplace to women's needs will also help retain females—in addition, policies such as flexible working, emergency childcare benefits and mental health support may help support the entire workforce, not just women.

Lastly, the report outlined that companies should focus on setting targets around fixing their broken pipelines. They should identify where their largest pipeline gap is in terms of promotions for women; for a lot of companies, this gap will be the first step up to becoming a manager. Once this gap is identified, companies should strive to put the same number of men and women up for promotion and try to root out gendered stereotypes, unconscious bias (which has most likely been a contributing factor to them having a higher percentage of male senior staff).

What Are Some Simple Strategies to Implement?

Some of the easy wins identified in the report include:

- Tracking differences in hiring and promotion rates between men and women.
- Setting clear and specific evaluation criteria for hiring.
- Sharing bias reminders prior to performance reviews and interviews.
- Providing regular unconscious bias training and track results.
- Sharing diversity metrics publicly.[81]

Conclusion from the McKinsey 2022 Report

'Women are more inclusive and empathetic leaders. They want to work for companies who are prioritising cultural changes that are improving work: flexibility, wellbeing, diversity, equity and conclusion. Companies that rise to the moment will attract and retain women leaders – and this will lead to a better workplace for everyone. They'll win the war for talent today and into the future'.

There Is a Glimmer of Light Sometimes

In November 2022, UEFA held the Convention on the Future of European Football in Nyon, Switzerland. What's this, I hear you cry? I'm not too sure, but Google told me this: *'Stakeholders from across the entire football community—national football associations, leagues, clubs, players, coaches, fans, agents, commercial partners and policymakers—held successful discussions focused on strengthening women's football, competitiveness and governance.'*

One of the outputs listed gave me a tiny twinkle of hope:

'A strong consensus was reached on the need to take stronger measures to increase gender balance in the higher instances of football's decision-making levels.'[82]

Unfortunately, nothing was written about exactly ***how*** they will do this, but at least it's out there that they agree they need to address it. It's a minor step in the right direction.

We Need to Fix Culture

United Kingdom Sport Chair, Dame Katherine Grainger, spoke during the 8th World Conference on Women and Sport in November 2022 in Auckland, New Zealand. Grainger raised multiple points, in particular:

'We need to act to make sure women are fairly represented in the room where all decisions on the future of sport are made. This means moving on from thinking we need to fix the women and instead focus more of our attention on fixing the culture. Rather than focusing just on upskilling women (who often already have the skills and experiences needed to succeed), we need to spend more time improving the culture of international sporting institutions to make sure they are supportive of and inclusive to women.

'We need to provide women with more opportunities to build the networks they will need to make progress in international sport leadership because we need more women in leadership positions to supercharge the power of high-performance sport to advance gender equality.'[83]

If we look at the world as a whole and scrutinise the leaders at the top who attended the COP27 summit held in Egypt in November

2022, just seven were women and 103 were men. BBC analysis found that women made up less than 34% of country negotiating teams at the meeting. And this was one of the lowest concentrations of women ever seen at these UN climate summits according to the Women's Environment and Development Organisation.[84]

We Must Keep Talking

I guarantee almost every girl or woman you know has walked purposefully across the road in fear of their safety, has walked home with their keys grasped in their hands, 'just in case', and has pretended to be on the phone not once, not twice, but multiple times in these situations.

I'm quite sure a lot of women reading this will have had at least one of the following said to them on more than one occasion … 'You're too loud. You're too emotional. You're too ambitious. You're too much. You're being difficult. You're so bossy.'

To all the women reading this, you're none of the above. 'You're brave. You're bold. You're assertive. And you're confident.'

Don't change a thing.

And yes, sexism will never go away completely, but let's not stop doing what we can. We can all take action. Forwards. Not backwards.

If we sit here in silence, nothing will change.

The Voice of Women Working in Sport Survey, 2023

An online survey was promoted via the Women's Sport Collective and wider sports industry in October 2022. It was completed by 863 women working in sport. Analysis and reporting were completed by Sporting Insights.

What were the key findings?

Almost none of the women who completed this research felt that there is gender equality in the sports industry. Scarily, the average gender equality score given by women working in the industry was only 4.63 out of 10.

What were the recommendations?

Improve gender equality in industry systems:

1. Increase the visibility of women working across all levels of sport.
2. Be more open-minded and transparent when recruiting.

3. Review pay and working conditions for gender bias.

Support women entering the industry:

1. Increase the number of women and girls positively engaged in sport.
2. Improve the awareness of sport as a career for women.
3. Encourage both sporty and non-sporty women into the industry.

Support women working in the industry:

1. Increase the number of male allies.
2. Provide formal mentoring opportunities.
3. Encourage and promote informal mentoring opportunities.[85]

And, We Need Action Now ... Because

In the last year alone, I, like many other women, experienced sexism on multiple occasions. In only the last couple of months, I have read numerous news stories from around the world about vile sexism and discrimination. Sexual assault. Racism. Anti-Semitism. Violence. Online abuse. And more. I struggle to understand why there are so many unkind people in this world, but the rise in hatred in the world is frightening.

In the last year, these things have been said to me:

- 'I bet you can't explain the offside rule.'
- 'You know a lot about football for a woman.'
- 'Give us a kiss, darling, you're beautiful.'
- 'How did you get a job at UEFA—who did you sleep with?'
- 'I can't wait to watch a game with you and hear your expert analysis, especially because you are a woman. I don't know any women who know anything about football. This is going to be fun.'
- 'Wow. You are the first woman I've met who knows anything about football. And you really know your stuff. I'm shocked.'
- 'Sally. Shut up. Get back to the kitchen. You sound like a broken record.'
- 'It is strange, because you are really pretty, and I don't associate pretty women with playing football. I have so many female clients, yet you are the first woman I know who loves football.'

Time and Time Again

I hear this nonsense. It's beyond exhausting, but for the record, I knew the offside rule when I was seven years old. I know a lot about football because I love it and I have followed it for years; played it, coached it, written about it, watched it all around the world and for a long time I was paid to work in it. I am not your darling. I will not give you a kiss. Ever. And I did not sleep with anyone.

I guess discrimination has always been there and maybe it feels like there is more right now due to news outlets reporting terrible stories more frequently. Either way, it appears there are a lot of unhappy people in the world. Add a two-year pandemic to the mix and voila—we might have had the recipe for a big 'perfect storm'.

Perhaps the social trauma we have experienced from lockdowns and their associated rules are a contributing factor; we have been somewhat forced to find new ways to vent our anger and frustration as we have been prevented from doing many things that typically offer emotional release and escapism. Does this make it OK? No.

Undeniably, governments worldwide will be dealing with the mental health consequences of lockdowns for years to come.

But we must stay strong and keep fighting. Why?

Because if we imagine a gender-equal world—a world free of bias, stereotypes and discrimination—a world that is diverse, equitable and inclusive—a world where difference is valued and celebrated, then it will be a better world than we live in right now.

And Never Forget. Gender Equality Is a Human Right

Gender equality is when people of all genders have equal rights, responsibilities and opportunities. It is a human right (Universal Declaration of Human Rights & Convention on the Elimination of All Forms of Discrimination against Women).[86]

In February 2023, António Guterres, the Secretary General of the United Nations, briefed the General Assembly on the importance of gender equality. He said:

'Half of humanity is held back by the most widespread human rights abuse of our time; women and girls in Afghanistan are exiles in

their own country, banned from public life, with every aspect of their lives controlled by men.

'As one young woman said: "We are dead, and yet alive."

'In Iran, women and girls have taken to the streets demanding fundamental human rights, at great personal cost. While the most extreme examples get attention, gender discrimination is global, chronic, pervasive and holds every single country back.

'And things are getting worse.

'At the international level, some governments now oppose even the inclusion of a gender perspective in multilateral negotiations.

'We face an intense pushback against the rights of women and girls.

'Women's sexual and reproductive rights and legal protections are under threat.

'I am frequently confronted with all-male panels—so-called "manels"—on issues that affect women and girls just as much as men and boys. These should be banned.

'Gender equality is a question of power.

''The patriarchy, with millennia of power behind it, is reasserting itself.

'The United Nations is fighting back and standing up for the rights of women and girls everywhere.'[87]

After the Final Whistle

The Accumulation Effects

When little things happen so regularly, they amass at an ominously rapid rate. One minute everything is calm, quiet and peaceful and then boom, shake, shake, shake the room—the tsunami hits with immense force, energy and acceleration. A drip on its own is just a drip. But when that drip becomes continuous, it can transform to an agonising flood. Cue an incoming, anxiety-fuelled, gut-wrenching tidal wave.

One thing in isolation can be really frustrating, and also more often than not, forgivable. But when one thing quickly becomes two, which turns to three, to four things that will likely, effortlessly snowball out of control, it's not forgivable.

For me, it came to the point where I had to say enough is enough. Respect was no longer being served—my own morals and ethics were coming into question almost daily and my mental health started to rapidly deteriorate. Quickly, my thinking changed, because quite simply, anything that costs your mental health is too expensive in my book and no job in the world is worth destroying yourself over even if you work in a beautiful place.

Why? Because even though society often tells us we must keep calm and carry on no matter what life throws at us, this isn't always necessarily for the best. In fact, I call it nonsense drivel. Why? Because it's absolutely essential (at times) and OK to pause. To stop. To take a breather. And in my experience, it takes far more courage and bravery to walk away than it does to stay.

Acceptance

After the mixed feelings of denial, frustration, sadness and anger, I began to slowly accept that while the powers that be are in the main unfit-for-purpose, male dinosaurs who sadly rot from the top, I would likely never be able to effect change. It was time to hold my head high, admit that I was broken and running on empty, and exit the revolving door, otherwise a full-on crash-and-burn moment was imminently looming.

Don't get me wrong, it was not an easy decision. I went back and forth with my thoughts time and time again. I explored countless ways to cling on, until the indecision started to drive me crazy. Shall I, shan't I? Maybe I can make this work. Shall I walk? Should I send the 'exit, I'm done, I'm out of here' email or should I wait a bit longer? I said to my friends it felt a bit like I was in denial. Deep down I knew what was wrong and what I needed to do. My instinct was telling me to leave and leave now, but they say love is blind; in this case, I was foolishly clinging on. I was a little blinded by reality and I kept finding reasons (albeit the wrong ones) to hold on—similar to how we know we shouldn't, but we still find a way to rationalise going back to an ex for sex!

Why Was It So Hard to Let Go?

Because it was my dream to work in football and I had worked incredibly hard to make it a reality. Football was and still is my number one passion. It is the biggest sport on the planet. I am devoted, enthusiastic and exceptionally knowledgeable about the beautiful game (modest too). And believe it or not, despite all the stories you have read, I do still love football more than most things!

Not many things are universal, but football is one. It is one of the most powerful, widespread languages in the world. What's another one? Food. Don't believe me?! Next time you get in a taxi, try it! I bet you will be able to strike (pun intended) up a conversation with the driver about football or food or both, no matter where in the world you are and no matter the language barrier.

Anyway, back on track. Why else was it so hard to let go?

I had worked so hard to get to this stage in my career, I'd been knocked back more times than I could remember, and I wanted to live my dream forever and ever and ever. I wanted, more than anything, for it to be the fairy tale and not the living nightmare I was experiencing. It's no wonder then that sometimes I would go into denial mode; I'd try to find another excuse or reason to stay, to fix things, and I'd hang on. I was like a jumping yo-yo, see-sawing between, 'I can't possibly walk away; this is my dream ... to ... if I don't walk away, the toxic, poisonous culture will most likely break me.'

When the latter thoughts dominated, I got clarity. No career is worth your health. I walked out. It hurt. I didn't want to admit failure. It felt like a break-up; my dream had been tainted. Maybe not quite extinguished, but it was badly bruised, and the hope of my football fantastical career started to fade faster than those oh-so-lovely, whiter-than-white bootcut jeans I owned in the 90s.

Onwards and Upwards

Better dreams are on their way. I am resolute. I am hopeful. I am positive. One door closes and another one opens. Who knows what is next on this wonderful rollercoaster ride that we call life! I'm sure there will be more ups and more downs, but I'm more than ready for the ride.

Let's never forget, football is for *everyone*. Football belongs to *all* those who love football. It is the most loved sport on the planet. It's magical. It brings hope. It brings screams of happiness and tears of joy. It keeps dreams alive, and it brings communities together all over the world. It's the most significant of all the unimportant things in life. It's a shared language with a global identity and quite often, football is a mirror of life.

So, let's not be shy and stay silent. The only wrong thing to say is to say nothing. To parents, guardians and anyone reading this—when you see sexism, please call it out. Please talk to your children about what is right and what is wrong. Why? Because they are the generation who will be able to influence change; they can be a force for good and their actions can and will make sexism dwindle.

As Anne Hathaway said, let's 'prioritise women for the good of all'.[88]

Acknowledgements

To the many people who have been with me on this challenging, thought-provoking writing journey—a massive thank you for listening to me rant, rave, scream, shout, cry and more. Thank you for being so incredibly generous with your time, patience and for also keeping me sane (*just about*)!

To those of you who read a chapter or two and provided honest, candid, wise feedback and anecdotes of your own personal experiences—thank you so much. Your astute and perceptive words, compassion and empathy meant the world—you kept me motivated at my low times and you ignited a little fire in my belly to keep going.

And massive heartfelt thanks too to the editor, to the designer, to the lawyer(s), to the photographer, to my publisher and the entire team behind the scenes who all contributed to magically making this waffle end up in a book! Now that I have some understanding of the multiple, complicated stages involved in writing one, I say chapeau, bravo and wow to all the authors out there who have written several books. I don't know how you did it—one has nearly killed me!

There were times when I thought I had bitten off more than I could chew. I laughed. I cried. I stopped. And yes, I came close to giving up. More than once. I contemplated throwing my laptop into Lake Geneva (I know, I'm mad), but thankfully, (I think), it never happened. Instead, I hammered the keyboard with fresh motivation, desire and an immense will to succeed.

So, next time you are in a bookshop and you pick up a book from the shelf—please take some time to think about the probable blood, sweat and tears that were shed to get it there. And please, don't be too quick to criticise the title, the cover, the wording or the layout. Believe me, it is far from easy.

Thank you to each and every one of you, from the bottom of my heart. I am forever grateful for your support and kindness.

Now it's time to celebrate. It is football and beer o'clock.

PS: Yes. I am a woman. And I like football and beer. Just saying...

Endnotes

[1] https://www.uefa.com/insideuefa/news/027b-16989ad91303-af64f152ea71-1000--top-european-club-coaches-attend-uefa-forum/

[2] https://fd.nl/opinie/1454863/is-de-parttime-werkende-vrouw-een-verwende-deeltijdprinses-of-eerder-een-assepoester

[3] https://asiapacific.unwomen.org/en/stories/speech/2022/11/unlocking-the-full-potential-of-women-in-the-economy

[4] https://www.linkedin.com/posts/european-commission_equalpay-unionofequality-genderpaygap-activity-6998321230881685504-AN1x?utm_source=share&utm_medium=member_desktop

[5] https://www.europarl.europa.eu/news/en/press-room/20221212IPR64524/gender-pay-gap-deal-reached-on-binding-pay-transparency-measures

[6] https://www.sbs.com.au/news/article/staggering-sexism-why-theres-backlash-over-coverage-of-jacinda-arderns-resignation/41sk82cxn

[7] https://journals.sagepub.com/doi/full/10.1111/j.1467-9280.2008.02079.x

[8] https://cultureplusconsulting.com/2018/03/10/gender-bias-work-assertiveness-double-bind/

[9] https://www.bbc.com/news/uk-politics-61247374

[10] https://www.independent.co.uk/voices/katharine-birbalsingh-hard-maths-phsyics-girls-gender-b2069312.html

[11] https://www.lbc.co.uk/news/cambridge-university-german-gender/

[12] https://www.bbc.com/news/health-63636201

[13] Ibid.

[14] https://www.theguardian.com/football/2022/sep/29/west-brom-women-switch-from-white-to-navy-shorts-due-to-period-concerns

[15] https://www.forbes.com/sites/asifburhan/2022/10/25/manchester-city-women-to-stop-wearing-white-shorts-over-period-concerns/?sh=315876e35458

[16] https://amp-theage-com-au.cdn.ampproject.org/c/s/amp.theage.com.au/sport/afl/an-awesome-outcome-white-shorts-ditched-for-aflw-players-to-ease-period-stress-20221207-p5c4lb.html

[17] https://edition.cnn.com/2020/12/02/football/stephanie-frappart-ucl-juventus-dynamo-kiev-spt-intl/index.html

[18] https://www.instagram.com/p/Clovb4QvHHU/?utm_source=ig_web_copy_link

[19] https://www.un.org/en/observances/womens-day

[20] https://www.linkedin.com/pulse/choosetochallenge-iwd2021-sally-freedman/

[21] https://en.wikipedia.org/wiki/2022_Finalissima

[22] https://en.wikipedia.org/wiki/2023_Women%27s_Finalissima

[23] https://www.un.org/sustainabledevelopment/wp-content/uploads/2018/09/Goal-5.pdf

[24] https://www.mckinsey.com/featured-insights/diversity-and-inclusion/diversity-wins-how-inclusion-matters

[25] https://www.skysports.com/football/news/19692/12485109/euro-2020-fa-review-on-wembley-final-disorder-finds-series-of-crowd-near-misses-which-could-have-led-to-fatalities

[26] https://www.bbc.com/sport/football/58360698

[27] https://theathletic.com/2704711/2021/07/15/this-is-what-you-endure-watching-england-as-a-woman-misogyny-sexism-and-the-constant-fear-of-being-touched-without-consent/?redirected=

[28] https://www.skysports.com/football/news/11095/12410072/gareth-southgate-says-there-are-not-enough-women-in-the-england-mens-national-team-set-up

[29] https://www.dw.com/en/germany-female-footballers-slam-sexist-punishment-for-soccer-coach/a-56941742

[30] https://www.irishpost.com/news/rugby-kit-manufacturer-under-fire-for-using-model-to-launch-ireland-womens-home-jersey-191812

[31] https://www.standard.co.uk/sport/rugby/rugby-world-cup-2022-england-women-rfu-economy-class-b1027724.html

[32] https://twitter.com/Bethany_Eng15/status/1558876297920745472?s=20&t=yXWG7kd-WwksP62mdbjDjg

[33] https://amp.theguardian.com/football/2022/jun/13/how-the-fa-banned-womens-football-in-1921-and-tried-to-justify-it

[34] https://www.bbc.com/sport/tennis/61675668

[35] https://twitter.com/JenShahade/status/1574805587027714050?s=20&t=NfqKezIlAq_rS7EkudA4Yw

[36] https://www.hrgrapevine.com/content/article/2022-11-03-virgin-atlantic-sees-job-applications-soar-after-scrapping-gendered-uniforms?utm_source=template-pardot-2202-v1&utm_medium=email&utm_campaign=hr-04-11-22&utm_content=news&utm_term=First+class+D%26I

[37] https://www.bbc.com/news/uk-scotland-60244442

[38] https://www.espn.co.uk/football/ajax/story/4588472/marc-overmars-leaves-ajax-after-appalling-message-scandal

[39] https://www.mirror.co.uk/news/politics/top-tory-caught-watching-porn-26810579

[40] https://globalnews.ca/news/8042726/beach-handball-bikini-bottom-shorts-women-norwegian/

[41] https://www.american.edu/cas/news/roe-v-wade-overturned-what-it-means-whats-next.cfm#:~:text=On%20Friday%2C%20June%2024%2C%202022,or%20outright%20ban%20abortion%20rights

[42] https://www.independent.co.uk/life-style/scotland-period-dignity-officer-man-backlash-b2146585.html

[43] https://www.beinsports.com/au/football/news/damning-report-on-us-womens-soccer/1961866

[44] https://finance.yahoo.com/news/nikita-parris-aims-euro-2022-182753799.html?guccounter=1&guce_referrer=aHR0cHM6Ly93d3cuZ29vZ2xlLmNvbS8&guce_referrer_sig=AQAAAEAePr1KrbQoU3aZ3Ru5TSNyF9GdaWRIAfnsMp-tiCIpoG0PIi8hs8-bkvlOnljhvOE7ARlELzXZy-EySXwQ65DUqZmcxMNzUC2nd460qTU6Bk4jHa9Ky4RghLvoeg8d2gv7J5n7Kmd31M4jmHiVGoaDxJsAKv5abAyaYVpCOTNm

[45] https://twitter.com/JudyMurray/status/1522611809529835520?s=20&t=gKkddjIbAnRcaQu5zapA0Q

[46] https://amp-theguardian-com.cdn.ampproject.org/c/s/amp.theguardian.com/football/blog/2022/apr/13/kenny-shiels-talk-of-emotional-women-is-unacceptable-football-deserves-better

[47] https://www.theguardian.com/education/2022/nov/18/eton-college-apologises-after-allegations-pupils-jeered-visiting-state-schoolgirls

[48] https://www.bbc.com/news/world-63803342

[49] https://www.theguardian.com/media/2022/dec/18/jeremy-clarkson-condemned-meghan-column-the-sun

[50] https://www.dailymail.co.uk/news/article-11554301/Jeremy-Clarkson-horrified-caused-hurt-column-Meghan-Markle.html

[51] https://www.bbc.com/news/uk-scotland-64000443

[52] https://www.theguardian.com/football/2023/mar/02/fifa-adriana-lima-supermodel-womens-world-cup-ambassador

[53] https://www.swissinfo.ch/eng/swiss-gender-pay-gap-among-the-widest-in-europe/48077132#:~:text=The%20gender%20pay%20gap%20in,work%2C%20according%20to%20new%20figures

[54] https://www.swissinfo.ch/eng/gender-equality-in-workplace-may-take--three-generations-/46948020?utm_campaign=teaser-in-article&utm_source=swissinfoch&utm_medium=display&utm_content=o

[55] https://www.linkedin.com/posts/akarpiak_very-popular-costume-this-year-activity-6991050931232481280-pcu_?utm_source=share&utm_medium=member_desktop

[56] *Invisible Women.* Caroline Criado Perez, Penguin Books Australia, page 108.

[57] https://www.bbc.com/worklife/article/20221021-the-bosses-who-silently-nudge-out-workers

[58] https://twitter.com/tracey_crouch/status/1553812417921970178

[59] https://www.skysports.com/football/news/11095/12828497/international-womens-day-girls-granted-equal-access-to-sport-as-lionesses-campaign-pays-off

[60] https://www.bbc.com/news/technology-63033078

[61] https://twitter.com/katieshanahan3/status/1552040002556657665?s=24&t=gzW12ai8xgfIgnZoHvXhGA

[62] https://bleacherreport.com/articles/10056166-world-cup-2022-prize-money-complete-purse-and-earnings-info-for-fifa-tournament

[63] https://www.tyla.com/news/womens-euros-2022-lionesses-prize-money-shocked-20220801?source=facebook&fbclid=IwAR1qpxrAdmKhzjzl2iwMzz2m62PSx3wLQFwFIe31XaVYB9ZxlpIDFZM_Psc&fs=e&s=cl

64 https://www.linkedin.com/posts/un-women_globalgoals-genderequality-activity-6985932305244504065-H0z3/?utm_source=share&utm_medium=member_desktop

65 *Invisible Women*. Caroline Criado Perez, Penguin Books Australia, page 8.

66 Ibid, page 11.

67 https://www.skysports.com/athletics/news/12040/12625206/sky-sports-news-investigation-finds-only-three-female-sport-statues-in-uk

68 *The People's Game,* Gary Neville, Hachette Australia, page 77.

69 https://www.espn.com.au/football/fifa-world-cup/story/4806837/pitfalls-in-fifa-presidents-speech-before-qatar-world-cup

70 https://time.com/6235503/one-love-armband-qatar-world-cup/

71 https://eu.usatoday.com/story/sports/soccer/worldcup/2022/11/21/iran-soccer-players-national-anthem-world-cup/10751171002/

72 https://twitter.com/em_sandy/status/1594638562993086469?s=20&t=7fVThmD5Yny7xPORfWYPAQ

73 https://www.jpost.com/international/article-722891

74 https://twitter.com/danielstorey85/status/1595403835098505216?s=48&t=76FylX6NLjyqz9nwkaXvkg

75 https://www.reuters.com/lifestyle/sports/germany-players-cover-mouths-team-photo-amid-armband-row-2022-11-23/

76 https://en.as.com/soccer/cristiano-ronaldo-becomes-the-first-player-to-score-in-5-separate-world-cup-finals-n/

77 https://twitter.com/diciccomethod/status/1599431078288429056?s=48&t=WEZxbOBE7MLC3O18H9pu_w

78 https://twitter.com/DiCiccoMethod/status/1599432158757949441?s=20&t=NyKjE_ZC9OVBrP4ytH0K3w

79 https://www.news.com.au/sport/football/gender-equality-behind-name-changes-of-aleague-and-wleague/news-story/297b2a46b7c86782c12874e5a61ea11f

80 https://www.bbc.com/news/uk-wales-64412891

81 https://www.linkedin.com/smart-links/AQEKI18yNxmdPA/55239142-6f15-4ea9-af28-103cfb04d83a

[82] https://www.uefa.com/insideuefa/news/027b-169067b195cc-4a7298a430b4-1000--stakeholders-agree-progress-on-competitiveness-women-s-football/?fbclid=IwAR0n1Ms30aT7hC65IvbvZyEucIUu8-GnTwUwLlRrtsNUPz4KyUXXEyY3gXSw

[83] https://www.linkedin.com/pulse/we-must-act-create-environment-high-performance-sport-where-women-/?trackingId=ARH9vVdJSlWvjQokPfPQnw%3D%3D

[84] https://www.instagram.com/p/ClB0_AwIpko/?utm_source=ig_web_copy_link

[85] https://www.sportinginsights.com/product/voice-of-women-working-in-sport/

[86] https://www.un.org/en/global-issues/gender-equality#:~:text=a%20human%20right-,Gender%20Equality%20was%20made%20part%20of%20international%20human%20rights%20law,Assembly%20on%2010%2-0December%201948

[87] https://www.un.org/sg/en/content/sg/statement/2023-02-06/secretary-generals-briefing-the-general-assembly-priorities-for-2023-scroll-down-for-bilingual-delivered-all-english-and-all-french-versions

[88] https://asiapacific.unwomen.org/en/stories/speech/2022/11/unlocking-the-full-potential-of-women-in-the-economy

Asian cup instagram
https://www.instagram.com/p/CMJbXQdgnCVEeRSo8mjvBQtJePrVktVuKEwQG40/

There's a broader point to be made
https://www.linkedin.com/posts/activity-6892407728371769344-pbEc?utm_source=share&utm_medium=member_desktop

Stephanie Frappart options
https://edition.cnn.com/2020/12/02/football/stephanie-frappart-ucl-juventus-dynamo-kiev-spt-intl/index.html
https://www.telegraph.co.uk/football/2020/11/30/stephanie-frappart-become-first-female-referee-officiate-mens/

UEFA and conmeebol
https://www.conmebol.com/pt-br/noticias-pt-br/conmebol-e-uefa-abrem-escritorio-de-representacao-conjunta-em-londres/

Female players don't look good enough to sell kits
https://www.thetimes.co.uk/article/female-players-don-t-look-good-enough-to-sell-kits-well-politely-look-at-lionel-messi-mb908p7nr

Spot the difference: Florence Williams on twitter
https://twitter.com/FlorenceW94/status/1297155751635492865?s=20

Bethany England
https://twitter.com/Bethany_Eng15/status/1558876297920745472?s=20

Women were banned
https://www.facebook.com/213122429084291/posts/-the-english-girls-are-working-wonders/1614509068945613/

Let the women play in more feminine clothes
http://www.thepostgame.com/blog/dish/201505/noted-chauvinist-sepp-blatter-dubs-himself-godfather-womens-soccer

Judy Murray
https://twitter.com/JudyMurray/status/1559629888965017600?s=20

Miedema
https://twitter.com/miedemastuff/status/1534502123840278528?s=20

Judy Murray
https://twitter.com/JudyMurray/status/1522611809529835520?s=20

One year to go celebrations
https://www.instagram.com/p/ByqD4v5iprYHyPVFktkyg7lAqn9H1AtsalmcZQ0/

Hiring manager who interviewed you
https://www.linkedin.com/posts/angiegarza_im-dying-activity-6991074463660339200-PdqU/?originalSubdomain=de

Vivienne Miedema
https://twitter.com/VivianneMiedema/status/1582329321397489664?s=20

UN
https://twitter.com/UN_Women/status/1570050815926370312?s=20

German football team silenced
https://twitter.com/danielstorey85/status/1595403835098505216

Ronaldo
https://twitter.com/goal/status/1591808109722234881?s=20

Google search results in many incorrect headlines:
https://www.google.com/search?q=cristiano+ronaldo+makes+history+as+first+player+to+score+in+five+world+cups+with+Ghana+-goal&source=lmns&bih=1024&biw=1920&rlz=1C1CSMH_deCH-1012CH1012&hl=en&sa=X&ved=2ahUKEwiFgZja28T-AhUZwwIHH-Q3zD3sQ_AUoAHoECAEQAA&bshm=bshqp/1

Ronaldo
https://sportstar.thehindu.com/football/fifa-world-cup/news/cristiano-ronaldo-first-to-score-in-five-fifa-world-cup-portugal-vs-ghana-qatar-2022/article66179508.ece

Ronaldo
https://www.reuters.com/lifestyle/sports/portugals-ronaldo-is-first-player-score-five-world-cups-after-goal-v-ghana-2022-11-24/

About the Author

Sally Freedman is an international sport industry expert.

She received the only full academic scholarship to study a Masters in Business (Sport Management) at Griffith University in Australia.

Since graduating, Sally has worked at an array of major sport events including the 2015 AFC Asian Cup, the 2018 Gold Coast Commonwealth Games, the UEFA Champions League and UEFA EURO 2020. Sally has worked in different areas including marketing, communication, fan engagement, protocol, ticketing and spectator services.

OTHER BOOKS FROM FAIR PLAY PUBLISHING

Hear Us Roar

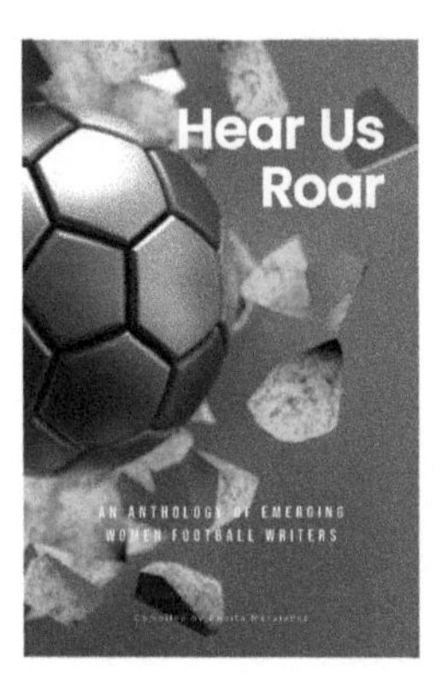

Encyclopedia of Matildas

Socceroos World Cup Odyssey

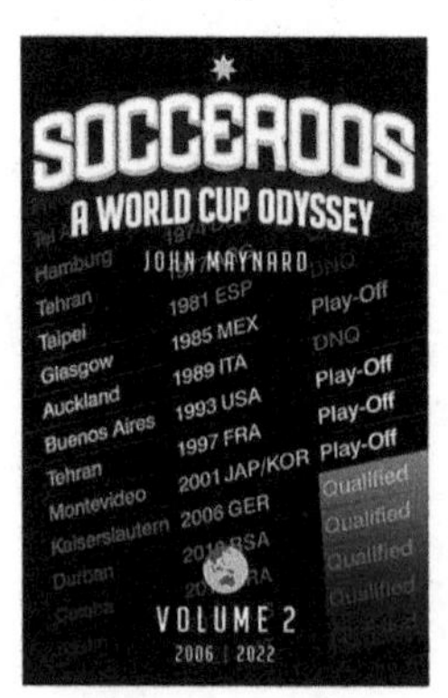

Green and Golden Boots

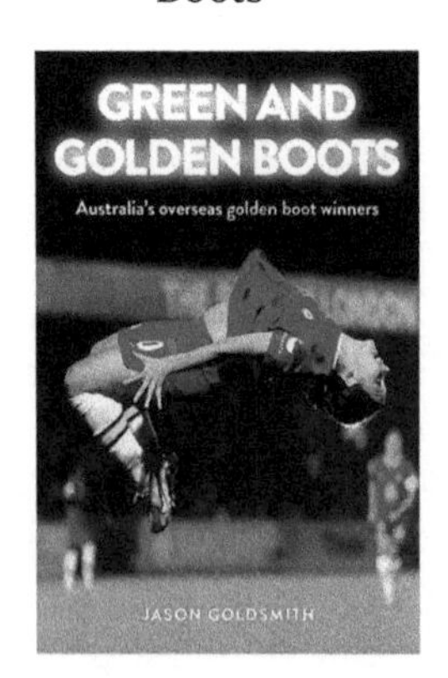

FAIRPLAY
PUBLISHING

Milton Keynes UK
Ingram Content Group UK Ltd.
UKHW022155200923
429077UK00011B/98